T0346654

GIDEON YEE SHUN TSANG

SUZANNE STABILE, SERIES EDITOR

FORTY DAYS ON

BEING A SEVEN

ENNEAGRAM DAILY REFLECTIONS

An imprint of InterVarsity Press
Downers Grove, Illinois

My life fell apart in 2019, and when I was all alone in the valley of the shadow of my grief, I found a friend there with me. David Whyte says, "Anything or anyone that does not bring you alive is too small for you." This book is dedicated to one of the true souls I have been honored to discover aliveness with: *Jason Minnix.*

◉ ◉ ◉ ◉

InterVarsity Press
P.O. Box 1400, Downers Grove, IL 60515-1426
ivpress.com
email@ivpress.com

InterVarsity Press® is the book-publishing division of InterVarsity Christian Fellowship/USA®, a movement of students and faculty active on campus at hundreds of universities, colleges, and schools of nursing in the United States of America, and a member movement of the International Fellowship of Evangelical Students. For information about local and regional activities, visit intervarsity.org.

All Scripture quotations, unless otherwise indicated, are taken from The Holy Bible, New International Version®, NIV®. Copyright © 1973, 1978, 1984, 2011 by Biblica, Inc.™ Used by permission of Zondervan. All rights reserved worldwide. www.zondervan.com. The "NIV" and "New International Version" are trademarks registered in the United States Patent and Trademark Office by Biblica, Inc.™

While any stories in this book are true, some names and identifying information may have been changed to protect the privacy of individuals.

The publisher cannot verify the accuracy or functionality of website URLs used in this book beyond the date of publication.

Enneagram figure by InterVarsity Press

Cover design and image composite: David Fassett
Interior design: Daniel van Loon
Images: gold foil background: © Katsumi Murouchi / Moment Collection / Getty Images
paper texture background: © Matthieu Tuffet / iStock / Getty Images Plus

ISBN 978-0-8308-4754-9 (print)
ISBN 978-0-8308-4755-6 (digital)

Printed in the United States of America ♾

InterVarsity Press is committed to ecological stewardship and to the conservation of natural resources in all our operations. This book was printed using sustainably sourced paper.

Library of Congress Cataloging-in-Publication Data
A catalog record for this book is available from the Library of Congress.

| P | 20 | 19 | 18 | 17 | 16 | 15 | 14 | 13 | 12 | 11 | 10 | 9 | 8 | 7 | 6 | 5 | 4 | 3 | 2 |
| Y | 37 | 36 | 35 | 34 | 33 | 32 | 31 | 30 | 29 | 28 | 27 | 26 | 25 | 24 | 23 | 22 | 21 |

WELCOME TO
ENNEAGRAM DAILY REFLECTIONS

Suzanne Stabile

The Enneagram is about nine ways of seeing. The reflections in this series are written from each of those nine ways of seeing. You have a rare opportunity, while reading and thinking about the experiences shared by each author, to expand your understanding of how they see themselves and how they experience others.

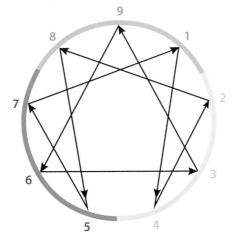

I've committed to teaching the Enneagram, in part, because I believe every person wants at least these two things: to belong, and to live a life that has meaning. And I'm sure that learning and working with the Enneagram has the potential to help all of us with both.

Belonging is complicated. We all want it, but few of us really understand it. The Enneagram identifies—with more accuracy than any other wisdom tool I know—why we can achieve belonging more easily with some people than with others. And it teaches us to find our place in situations and groups without having to displace someone else. (I'm actually convinced that it's the answer to world peace, but some have suggested that I could be exaggerating just a bit.)

If our lives are to have meaning beyond ourselves, we will have to develop the capacity to understand, value, and respect people who see the world differently than we do. We will have to learn to name our own gifts and identify our weaknesses, and the Enneagram reveals both at the same time.

The idea that we are all pretty much alike is shattered by the end of an introductory Enneagram workshop or after reading the last page of a good primer. But for those who are teachable and open to receiving Enneagram wisdom about each of the nine personality types, the shock is accompanied by a beautiful and unexpected gift: they find that they have more compassion for themselves and more grace for others and it's a guarantee.

The authors in this series, representing the nine Enneagram types, have used that compassion to move toward a greater understanding of themselves and others whose lives intersect with theirs in big and small ways. They write from experiences that reflect racial and cultural differences, and they have been influenced by different faith beliefs. In working with spiritual directors, therapists, and pastors they identified many of their own habits and fears, behaviors and motivations, gifts and challenges. And they courageously talked with those who are close to them about how they are seen and experienced in relationship.

As you begin reading, I think it will be helpful for you to be generous with yourself. Reflect on your own life—where you've been and where you're going. And I hope you will consider the difference between change and transformation. *Change* is when we take on something new. *Transformation* occurs when something old falls away, usually beyond our control. When we see a movie, read a book, or perhaps hear a sermon that we believe "changed our lives," it will seldom, if ever, become transformative. It's a good thing and we may have learned a valuable life lesson, but that's not transformation. Transformation occurs when you have an experience that changes the way you understand life and its mysteries.

When my dad died, I immediately looked for the leather journal I had given to him years before with the request that he fill it with stories and things he wanted me to know. He had only written on one page:

*Anything I have achieved or accomplished
in my life is because of the gift of your mother
as my wife. You should get to know her.*

I thought I knew her, but I followed his advice, and it was one of the most transformative experiences of my life.

From a place of vulnerability and generosity, each author in this series invites us to walk with them for forty days on their journeys toward transformation. I hope you will not limit your reading to only your number. Read about your spouse or a friend. Consider reading about the type you suspect represents your parents or your siblings. You might even want to read about someone you have little affection for but are willing to try to understand.

You can never change *how* you see, but you can change what you *do* with how you see.

ON BEING A SEVEN

Several years ago, I encountered the Enneagram test for the first time like I was sitting in the back row in high school—disinterested to say the least. Test? Lame. What is this, a horoscope? Lame. *Another* personality test? I hate tests and I dislike being put into boxes.

But fine, whatever, I'll do it. I'll appease you by taking this multiple-choice test, but in my mind it will have zero stakes. Will I pass? How do I succeed? There are nine types? Why nine? I'm a Seven? Cool. Whatever. What's for lunch?

A year later, our leadership team decided to take the test again. *Not again!* I thought to myself.

"It will help us know each other's strengths and weaknesses better!"

"It will give us common language!"

Fine. I relented.

We sat on the front porch of a ranch in Dripping Springs, Texas. This time we delved into each type more deeply. I tried to remember my test result from the previous year. Because I cared so little, I couldn't recall it.

The presenter started to give examples of famous people from each type. Type One, the Perfectionist? Nope. Type Two, Helper? Nah. Type Three, Achiever? Negative. Type Four, the Romantic? Ohhh, I want to be a romantic.

The presenter listed off a few names—Bob Dylan, Alan Watts, Leonard Cohen, and *Thomas freaking Merton?* Please, please, please let me be a Four.

I missed the explanation of the next few numbers trying to do the mental Pilates needed to cram my obviously non-Four existence into a Romantic Four box. Am I melancholy? Once a decade, perhaps. That probably counts. Do I ruminate on my feelings? What are feelings?

The presenter then came to the Seven, the Optimist. The description started with everything I find embarrassing. Sevens are hyper-positive! Sevens are childlike! They love to party and avoid pain! They are easily distracted! They will text with lots of exclamation points! Because they go through life seeking more exclamation! My eyes rolled to the back of my head so far they came right back around like a scene from *The Exorcist*.

As the presenter listed off famous Sevens, I felt a resistance building to this demonic number. "Famous Sevens are . . . Miley Cyrus! Charlie Sheen! Britney Spears!" *Noooo!* That's it. No matter what anyone says, *I am not a Seven!* I had decided right then and there. Anything but a Seven. So back to the Four . . .

Later that year, I got a text message on a Wednesday afternoon. I felt the buzz in my back left pocket. I reached for my phone and saw it was from my friend Chris, whom I hadn't seen in years. "Wanna hang with Father Richard Rohr for three days in Santa Fe?" he asked.

I didn't ask for more details or the price or even the dates and responded, "Hell, yeah! I'm on my way!" (In hindsight, perhaps the most textbook Seven response possible.)

Chris texted back, "Umm . . . I meant in six months."

Oh. I'll start walking then.

Six months later, we spent a weekend in a beautiful hotel in downtown Santa Fe with one of my living man crushes. On the second day, Rohr spent the morning teaching us the Enneagram. Hearing the description from someone I respected deeply finally gave me the courage to accept the embarrassing parts of myself. Fine. I'm a Seven.

After the session, there was a coffee break. People stretched and grabbed drinks, and I wandered over to my man crush to make small talk. Rohr looked at me with kind eyes and asked, "So, Gideon, what type do you think you might be?"

I smiled, finally accepting my Enneagram fate, and confidently said, "I believe I'm a Seven, Richard."

He turned and looked at me like he was deep in thought. "Hmmm," he said. "Really? You don't feel like a Seven to me."

Immediately I was thrown into an existential crisis. Richard Rohr doesn't think I'm a Seven! *Who am I?*

These days I've come to accept that I am a Seven—but an Asian Seven. Consider me a Seven with the triple repression of Chinese stoicism mixed with a fundamentalist upbringing and a Canadian apology for my existence. I'm so sorry I'm a Seven, eh?

I've also learned the following truths about myself through the Enneagram:

- Even though I don't look like I have anxiety and can project confidence in the world, my anxiety is like a low-grade fever that affects most of my decisions.

- My hyper-positivity is a protector that has shielded me from half of my reality.

- I like options and can live in the gray pretty well except under stress. Under stress, everything becomes black and white.

- When I am not stressed, I can delve into an interest in a deep way. I read more when I'm not stressed. I can sit with a poem for an entire day when I'm relaxed.

- My addiction to being liked is exhausting. It started with some early childhood wounds that I'm now learning to nurture as an adult.

- I have a hard time liking myself and so need the external world to validate me (and by external world I mean everyone I ever meet. Seriously. Makes me want to nap).

- Adventure and exploration are my happy place.

- I bring a lightness to a situation that is a gift.

- My openness to options looks like me changing my mind a lot. That stresses people out.

A few years later I was with Richard Rohr again (full disclosure: Sevens like to name-drop. I get super annoyed when other Sevens do it and then catch myself doing the same thing. *Grrrrr*), this time at his office in Albuquerque. We had finished a day together and I found him sitting in his office. He could see the spark of mischief in my eyes.

"May I ask a favor, Richard?"

"Sure, Gideon. What does the Seven in you need?"

"Could we take a Boomerang for my Instagram story?"

"I don't know what those words mean, Gideon. But whatever will make the Seven in you happy."

"Oh, this will, Richard. OK, let's hold hands, and don't smile. On the count of three hold up the peace sign. Ready? One . . . two . . . three."

◉ ◉ ◉ ◉

The Scriptures talk about God knowing us so intimately that God knows the number of hairs on our head. That's deeply intimate because that number changes every day. God has always known the parts of myself that embarrass me. I'm trying to allow myself to be loved into loving even those parts.

Whether you are a Seven or you want to explore how to better love a Seven in your life, I invite you to come along with me on a journey into the life of a Seven. At the end of each reading you'll find an invitation to reflect or pray or pick up a new spiritual practice as well.

Ready? One . . . two . . . three.

WHERE ARE YOU FROM?

I'VE ALWAYS BEEN FASCINATED by Jesus' statement of homelessness in Luke 9:58, where he says, "Foxes have dens and birds have nests, but the Son of Man has no place to lay his head." Perhaps Jesus is inviting us to find home within. If we can be at home anywhere, we can be at home everywhere.

I've actually been searching for home all my life. I was born in Saskatoon, Saskatchewan, and by the time I was twenty-five, "home" had been eight different cities. Then I landed in Austin, Texas, and I've been here for twenty years now.

At the end of a recent eight-week jaunt around the country, my family cheered when we pulled our camper onto our street. We hugged and high-fived. We were hugging and high-fiving for a sense of home. For the neighbors we've seen grow up and move off to college. For the coffee shop, bar, and restaurant owners who built this neighborhood together with us. For our friends and acquaintances. Whoops and hollers. We were finally home.

Occasionally, however, I am reminded that I'm still not

completely at home in Austin. This happens to me about once a year.

A few months ago I was sitting at a bodega in my neighborhood called Quickie Pickie. I was enjoying a Topo Chico while finishing some work at a table on the patio. I noticed in my peripheral vision a man staring at me. After a few minutes he was still staring, so I glanced over and we made eye contact. I smiled and looked back at my MacBook. Another few minutes and he was still looking at me, so I smiled and waved. He took that as a sign to get up and come over to my table. He introduced himself as Gary and asked me the question all people of color love to be asked: "Where are you from?"

With an internal eye roll I responded, "I've lived in Austin for twenty years. I think I can say Austin is home."

"Where are you from, though?"

"Well, I moved here from Detroit."

"I mean, where are you *really* from?"

"I lived in Chicago before that."

"Seriously, where are you *from* from?"

"OK, you got me. I'm from Canada."

He then proceeded to tell me a long story about his trip to Japan and his Japanese friend. I listened to his entire way-too-long story because I'm polite and Canadian. At the end I said, "Cool story. I'm not Japanese and I've never been to Japan."

He walked away confused.

As a Seven who's done chasing and moving, I've continued to ask questions about home. I've realized that as I've moved and traveled around the world, I've been running from asking myself who I am. Sevens will visit any other place rather than be at home with themselves.

So what *does* it mean to be at home with myself? For me it means exploring underlying questions such as: What does it look like for a Chinese Canadian to be at home in Austin? When did I start to assimilate and externalize my sense of home? What's the appropriate amount of space for a Chinese Canadian man to take up in the world? Why do I apologize so compulsively—am I apologizing for my existence? How can I be at home with the paradox that I'm not that important *and* I am the glory of God?

What does it mean for you to be home with yourself?

What other questions emerge as you consider that question?

RE-NURTURE

THEY SAY SEVENS' CORE WOUND is the fact that nurturing was withdrawn from them too early in life. I think about this often and how it has shaped me as an adult.

My father (an Enneagram Eight) has shared many stories of how he learned to fight for his life. So it's only natural that he would love me by challenging me to do the same. When I was five years old we lived in Paramaribo, Suriname. Every Monday we went to a fancy resort where the expats clustered. It was there that my father taught me how to swim.

Not long ago he asked my own teenage boys, "Want to hear how I taught your dad to swim?"

"Uh, sure."

"We were at this nice pool we went to every week. Your dad always refused to go into the deeper water."

"Because he was five years old, right?" my boys replied.

"Well, he needed to be more brave."

"But wasn't he just five?"

"He was ready. Your dad was having too much fun in the shallow end. He was ready for deeper water. So I asked, 'Hey, Gideon, would you like a Coke?' He said, 'Yeah! I love Coke!'"

"Dad was drinking Coke at five? No wonder you're so short, Dad. Ha-ha."

I couldn't help but grin. It gives me great joy when my boys feel safe enough to talk trash to me.

"So your dad got up out of the water and we were walking along the side of the pool to the bar. As soon as we got to the deepest part of the pool, I elbowed him in! He landed face first. He started flailing. He cried for help. And I didn't help him! I knew he could do it. He splashed his way back to the edge of the pool. And now he can swim!"

"Man, that story's messed up. Do you remember that, Dad?"

"For some reason I don't. Seems like that memory's been blocked."

"Sorry, Dad. I'm glad you didn't teach us to swim like that."

My father finished his story proudly: "Your dad's such a strong swimmer now."

I love my dad. I'm impressed with how he survived and thrived through many hardships. And when I find myself in over my head, I know how to look ahead and survive. Yet I also learned to avoid pain in my life because I'm too ready to be shoved into things at any moment without warning. In many ways this is my Seven origin story. I am resilient and slow to my emotion in equal parts.

> Read this verse: "Just as Jesus was coming up out of the water, he saw heaven being torn open and the Spirit descending on him like a dove. And a voice came from

heaven: 'You are my Son, whom I love; with you I am well pleased'" (Mark 1:10-11).

Now rewrite the last sentence: "(your name), you are my child, whom I love; with you I am well pleased."

Say this statement slowly. Savor the words. Notice what comes up as you place the words gently on your heart. Write out any insights you notice. Repeat the statement slowly three more times. Each time allow yourself to linger on a different insight.

CHASING APPROVAL

I HAVE TWO MEMORIES OF MY FATHER coming to my basketball games. So when he showed up to one of my games my junior year of high school, it was a big deal. I remember getting the ball tipped to me on the first play. I drove the ball and got fouled as I scored the layup. I hit the free throw and scored the game's first three points.

It was by far the best basketball half I've ever played. I scored eighteen points but also fouled out with two minutes to go in the half. I was too excited to control all of my adrenaline. I remember sitting on the bench excited that I'd scored eighteen points but embarrassed that I'd fouled out.

During the car ride home, my entire conversation with my father was about why I fouled so much. He didn't mention any of the points I'd scored.

I can only now access the sadness I must have felt then. I know my father has always loved me, and as a parent now myself, I often find myself missing him. I know he was doing his best. But it still stung.

In 2011 I took my first sabbatical as a pastor. I was fourteen years in, burnt and crispy like bread left in a toaster too long. I sat in a therapist's office for the first time.

"I don't want to be a pastor anymore."

"Why do you think you became a pastor?"

"I think I'm a frustrated idealist and also codependent. I'm addicted to rescuing people so that they'll love me or so I can feel worthy of love. I don't want to do that anymore."

"What do you think is underneath that?"

"Honestly, I think I wanted my parents to love me for who I was. I could never do well enough to earn that. I wasn't smart enough in school, athletic enough in sports, compliant enough to follow all their rules, moral enough to fit into fundamentalism. Weird, I thought that all went away when I became a pastor. But I think I became a pastor because I wanted my father to love me."

"How does it feel to say that out loud?"

"It's a lot to process. I think it's possible that all the validation I've been needing from my congregants is probably about my dad."

Wow. I've pastored for decades because I wanted my dad to approve of me. Since that time our relationship has healed tremendously. I love my father and I know he loves me.

Before Jesus' ministry began, his hippie off-the-grid cousin John baptized him (see Mark 1). The heavens opened and Jesus received validation and love from his Father. "This is my son, and he's loved."

The validation, love, and approval came before Jesus accomplished anything. Jesus began his three years of ministry out of love.

I wake up each morning and do the meditation I shared in Day Two. I ask to receive the words offered to Jesus for all of us: "This is my son, and he is loved." "This is my daughter, and she is loved."

How can I live out of love today instead of living to be loved? Often my actions are the same either way, but they come from different places in my soul.

Do something or imagine doing something in order to be loved more. Notice how that energy feels in your body. Notice the place it comes from.

Do something or imagine doing something out of a sense of being deeply loved and accepted. (Refer to the Day Two meditation if needed.) Notice how that energy feels in your body. Notice the place it comes from.

BELONGING EXHAUSTION

SEVENS ARE GOOD AT HAVING many acquaintances. Acquaintances are different from friendships. As a result, we can be very social and still not feel like we belong.

I moved to Toronto in the middle of my freshman year of high school. It was my fourth move in five years. I showed up on my first day without a school-sanctioned uniform. I walked through a sea of gray pants and white polos in my bright-yellow sweatshirt. I felt like Moses parting a sea of Canadian teenagers, all turning their heads to look at the weird new kid. As I passed, groups of cliques went back to their giggling and gossip as the metal lockers clanged shut.

That confirmed it: I didn't belong. I was an Asian kid in a white high school. I didn't belong. I was a short kid who loved to play basketball. I didn't belong. I was a Protestant kid in a Catholic high school. I didn't belong. I was a Chinese kid who wasn't good at math. I *definitely* didn't belong.

After several painful weeks, I finally made a friend named Mark. One day during lunch he looked across his plate of French fries and gravy and invited me to a party at his house that night. I looked behind me, unsure who he was talking to. "You want *me* to come to *your* party?" Knowing that all the cool kids would be there, I said yes.

I ran home that afternoon, bursting through the front door, proclaiming my life-changing news. "Who has two thumbs and got invited to a party? This guy!" I announced.

My fundamentalist immigrant parents were wary of all things worldly. I could tell by their silence and lack of eye contact that this announcement scared them. Who knew how much corruption Canadians kids could brainwash into their son in one drunken freshman party? "You're not going," they declared.

But this was my only chance. I would not let my sliver of social hope die. "I *am* going!" After hours of protest and personal activism, my parents relented with a strict curfew of 10 p.m.

I remember walking down the stairs into the basement of Mark's house. The first two hours of the party were an exercise in postpubescent awkwardness. A basement full of teenagers sat around staring at their feet. Finally, someone turned up the music and the party started bumping. I looked at my watch—9:45 p.m. I needed to be home in fifteen minutes. I had a decision to make. I could stay at the party and finally make some friends or go home and slumber in my social abyss. I stayed until midnight.

Two strangers dropped me off in front of my house. The lights were off—not a good sign. I fumbled in the dark and turned my key to unlock the door. The handle did not budge. It was deadbolted from the inside. I knocked quietly, hoping to awaken my sisters without my parents noticing. It finally sunk in. I was locked out of the house. This was the nail in the coffin. I didn't even belong in my own home.

I sat on my front lawn staring into the darkness. After several minutes I got up and started to wander. I was alone for the next eight hours. As I walked up and down the streets in the suburban silence, past identical brick houses, groomed lawns, and three-foot trees, I remember loneliness having a palpable weight to it. I can still feel it today.

It dawned on me that night. If I didn't get my act together, this was what the rest of my life would be like. That night set the trajectory for the next thirty years. As a Seven, I can curate my life to look externally impressive, yet I'm simply asking the same question: Will you accept me? Do I belong?

We all carry a story of belonging. Take a moment to reflect on your own story, and then write a page of reflection titled, "My Belonging Journey." Include significant memories of exclusion and inclusion.

Consider ways you take up space in community.

What vulnerable edges did you discover?

How can you carry those vulnerabilities and invite God and community to support you?

BEFRIENDING MY ANXIETY

I DON'T HAVE ANXIETY; I HAVE IDEAS!

I don't have anxiety; I like to have lots of fun in different ways, constantly!

I don't have anxiety; sometimes I just can't stop coming with the jokes!

Ohhh . . . maybe I have anxiety. (Sevens' anxiety comes with a lot of jokes.)

Since that realization I've spent years judging my anxiety, which is super helpful by the way. If you're into self-defeating circular exercises, I highly recommend it.

I grew up in a household with two sisters, Rachel and Hannah. Then, when I was ten years old, two cousins named Fanny and Lilian joined the crew. (Despite sounding like retired ladies in their seventies, these cousins were from Hong Kong and in high school.)

One particular evening I was in our basement surrounded by four women. As a ten-year-old I didn't mind at all—I liked any party. I remember the sounds of laughter, stories being told, jokes with punchlines. I also remember not being wanted. "Go away, Gideon! You're *sooo* annoying."

For an Enneagram Seven, not being wanted at the party is hell on earth. I don't remember what I said or did. I imagine a ten-year-old boy's capacity to respond in an emotionally sophisticated way is about like a puppy's ability to eat politely off the dinner table. I said something that must have been abrasive, and it earned me an open-handed slap to the face.

That was one of my first memories of trying to stand up for myself. The result? I got slapped for it. Since then I've lived my life wondering if God will also slap me in the face when I stand up for myself. It's a low-grade emotional fever that's followed me for thirty-five years. Even today it takes concentration and effort to stand up for myself. I catch myself emotionally flinching and ducking, then opening my eyes and realizing I'm an adult now. There's no one out to hit me, especially not God.

In fact, time and again Scripture goes out of its way to remind us that the converse is true. God hasn't ever left us. We've never been alone any of those days when we were crippled by anxiety. Sometimes I wonder how many crippled people in the Gospels were victims of anxiety. Jesus reminds us that perfect love casts out all fear (1 John 4:18). We're loved and loved and loved until our anxiety trusts that we can relax into that love. Occasionally I even find myself being courageous and living without anxiety. Very occasionally.

As a middle-aged man, I've befriended my anxiety. I've named him Frank. His full name is Frankxiety. Throughout my life, Frank has been a good friend. Most of the time he was simply trying to keep me from getting hit in the face. We've talked, and Frank understands that I'm no longer ten years old. He's still there if I need him but, in the meantime, I get to drive. He's in charge of the jokes.

Try centering prayer for five minutes. Choose a word to return to. I like to use the words "still," "here," or "compassion." Every time a thought arises, gently come back to your word.

What do you notice about your thoughts and anxiety?

How does it feel to rest simply in yourself?

BEFRIENDING MYSELF

IN THE SCRIPTURES, KING DAVID calls God "the LORD of hosts" (Psalm 24:10 ESV). Like God is the host of the best party. I imagine what it would be like to go to Oprah Winfrey's mansion for a party. *Everybody gets a hug!* I bet Oprah can hold court in her house like a G. The Scriptures remind us that God is holding court inside us, welcoming us to be with ourselves.

Now the catch here is that being present with myself isn't all that enjoyable. I recently heard the comedian Neal Brennan talk about how if we met someone on the street who said the things our inner critic says, we'd punch him in the face. I opened up my inner critic journal and read a few things I had written down.

"You'll never be loved."

"You're too much for people."

"Why are you so needy?"

"This book you're writing is going to be an embarrassment."

Yup, my inner critic is punch-worthy for sure.

David, in Psalm 84:10, says, "Better is one day in your courts than a thousand elsewhere." I used to read this psalm as a kid and feel confused. I could literally think of a thousand places I'd rather be than in church. How much boredom could I endure before I stabbed someone? Shouldn't the psalm read, "Better is one day at the beach" or "at an amusement park" or "at the candy store" or "sleeping in my bed"?

It dawned on me recently that David might have been saying it was better to be where God dwells—*in us*—for one day than a thousand elsewhere. Better is one day present to ourselves and to God in us than a thousand elsewhere.

Last week I had a rare day. I woke up and spent twenty minutes in centering prayer, made myself a steak and salad for lunch, then went on a hike and a bike ride. That night I sat in my Eames chair listening to a record. For some reason my inner protectors and managers were off duty. I took a deep breath and said aloud (to myself, I guess), "Today was a good day. I enjoyed being myself today. Gideon Yee Shun Tsang, you are a good hang."

I don't get there often, but when I do, it's better than a thousand days elsewhere.

What ways do you avoid being with yourself?

When was the last time you enjoyed the fullness of who you are—both your light and your shadows?

LEARNING CONFLICT

THIRTY-FIVE YEARS AGO I WENT to a Christian school in Calgary, Alberta. My working class parents spent our college tuition money to drive us from our lower-middle-class neighborhood forty-five minutes across town to receive an education with all the rich, white kids. My sister, her friend Tara, and I were the diversity in the school.

There was a kid in my class named Shaun. Our parents were on the same pickup schedule. His dad would pull into the parking lot in a Mercedes convertible with sunglasses on, a polo shirt with a popped collar, and a sweater draped around his shoulders. He looked like he'd driven off the set of *Pretty in Pink* to pick up his ten-year-old son. Often behind him was my refugee immigrant father in a white Hyundai Pony. You've probably never heard of this car because the United States of America took one look and rejected it like Dikembe Mutombo in an NBA game. Canada, on the other hand, said, "We'll take it, eh?" Then politely apologized for nothing. It's the Canadian way. You could buy a Hyundai Pony new for 5,795 Canadian dollars (probably about 50 dollars US) in the 1980s.

One day during recess, Shaun lost his preppy mind and called me a "little chink." "Go back to China!" he yelled.

I charged him. "I've never even been to China, you asshole!"

The teacher quickly pulled us apart and only I was sent to the principal's office. Apparently it was appropriate to call someone a chink but not an asshole.

The clean-cut, mustached principal in a suit handed me a combo platter of disdain and disappointment with a sprinkling of condescension. He instructed me to hold out my hand and asked me if I understood what I had done wrong. Then he hit me with a leather strap he took off his Bible.

Holding back tears, I nodded yes. Internally I was screaming, *I was trying to stand up for myself!* I didn't realize at the time that I was experiencing the complexity of being a kid of color in white Canada. The message I received was loud and clear: if you stand up for yourself, you will be punished.

When I read in the Scriptures that God stands up for injustice, my mind agrees but my heart doesn't always believe that to be the case. As a child, I never thought of myself as the poor, lame, leper, or widow that God had utter empathy for. But as an adult, I am slowly able to see that God was weeping with me on that day. I was being bullied by white Christian culture for the color of my skin.

As a Seven, I sit with that and see God's utter compassion for my fear of conflict and rejection. Experiencing that compassion slowly gives me the courage to engage conflict and the possibility of not being liked in my life today. Very, very, very slowly.

Do you remember a time you tried to stand up for yourself and it didn't go well?

How does it feel knowing that God stands with you in the injustice you've experienced in life?

PRESENT TO BEING ALMOST THERE

FOUR YEARS AGO MY RAGTAG CYCLING CLUB started a New Year's Day bike race called Red Rock Roubaix. It starts in Austin and traverses 113 miles of countryside roads. This past January we had 140 riders participate, from Tour de France professionals to casual Freds on hybrid bikes.

At 7 a.m. we were led out by my friend Spencer on a dirt bike. Five miles out of town, the moto peeled off and the race was on. The professionals in the front started attacking the early climbs. This asphyxiated the rest of us, who stretched into a long string of riders hanging on for dear life.

Twenty miles into the race, I checked my heart rate. It was a casual . . . 190! I still had ninety miles to go! I sat up, knowing a group of homies were behind me. As my heart slowly calmed down from its state of panic, I heard the familiar hum of a bike, coupled with laughter and conversation. A group of twenty smiling friends came riding by with waves and blown kisses.

"Hop on, Gideon!"

For the next eighty miles we rode under the sun on some of central Texas's finest paved and gravel roads. We reached a store in Manor, Texas—our final rest stop—at about 2 p.m. Everyone was basking in the endorphins in our brains, the lactic acid screaming in our legs, and the tallboys in our hands. After ten minutes of enjoying myself and halfway through my beer, I started to feel antsy. We were celebrating like we'd arrived, but in reality we still had ten miles to ride. We were so close to home! We were almost there!

The Irish poet and philosopher David Whyte has a poem called "Close," where he describes how feeling "almost there" is the truest of human experiences.

What I often forget to remember is that being at that store ten miles away—almost there—is life itself. As a Seven, my brain is always in the future imagining that the finish will feel more satisfying or more real. In reality, being almost there is as true and present as being thirty minutes away.

That day I rushed a small group of us back on our bikes to hammer home. It was ten miles. I could have savored the quiet country roads, making eye contact with alpacas with the seventy-degree sunshine kissing my face. Instead I rode with my head down, eyes crossed, pounding my way home. I crossed the finish line spent and exhausted.

Thirty minutes later the tallboy crew came rolling in, all smiles and high-fives. They had cruised and laughed their almost there-ness to the finish. And I had missed it.

I think about every generation after Jesus' ascension waiting for the kingdom of God to arrive. Perhaps the kingdom of God is available here and now if we understand that we're almost there. That's probably why Jesus said the kingdom of heaven is within us (Luke 17:21 KJV). Perhaps we experience God's kingdom not in our arrival but in our present journey.

As a youngster I thought there would be a day when I arrived. But now I wonder if "arrival" is the practice of being present to being almost there.

> I find Thich Nhat Hanh's breathing exercise helpful to bring me into the present. Try it throughout the day:
>
> Breathing in, I calm my body.
> Breathing out, I smile.
> Dwelling in the present moment,
> I know this is a wonderful moment.

THE BEAUTY
OF IMPERFECTION

SEVENS ARE FRUSTRATED IDEALISTS. We have an overly optimistic picture of the world. If I can just be positive enough and work hard enough, I can control everything to make it as close to perfect as possible.

Of course, this is simply a fantasy and a stressful way to live. Sevens take on the unhealthy characteristics of the Enneagram One under stress. I have lived most of my vocational life under stress. As a lousy perfectionist.

In Michelle Obama's documentary *Becoming*, she talks about how she got on Air Force One for the last time and wept for thirty minutes straight. She described the release she felt after eight years of trying to be perfect while the entire world was watching. I ain't no Michelle Obama, but I found that surprisingly relatable. Our beauty is not in unattainable perfection—it is that we are made in the image of God. We are beautiful simply as we are, with all of our light and shadows.

The band of followers Jesus chose to lead his revolution of love was far from perfect. It's as if Jesus went out of his way to show us the beauty and the messiness of their full humanity. Matthew—a turncoat who exploited a marginalized people for tax dollars? Beautiful. Thomas—a skeptic who lacked the faith to fully trust Jesus' revolution of peace? Beautiful. Peter—a loudmouthed, impulsive erratic who declared perfect loyalty to Jesus and ended up publicly disowning him? Beautiful.

I think it's possible that the storytellers are trying to point to a beauty greater than perfection. That we are fully loved in our flawed beauty.

After the resurrection, we follow the story of Jesus having breakfast on the beach with Peter. I imagine Peter being flooded with shame, waiting for an admonition. Instead of rebuke, he is met simply with love. Sometimes it makes me sad that Judas killed himself before seeing that he was loved even with his mistakes and imperfections. I wish Judas had breakfast on the beach too.

After Enneagram Ones, Sevens might be the hardest on themselves, striving for a perfection that doesn't exist and that no one asked for. I hope that I can continue to fail my way into my beauty.

Why are we so afraid to fail?

What do you think would happen if you failed?

When you are confronted with your flaws, imagine Jesus meeting you with tenderness and mirroring your beauty back to you.

CRUSHED INTO BECOMING

IN HIGH SCHOOL I HAD A HUGE CRUSH on a girl named Kirsten Philips. She was slim with dark-blond hair pulled back in a ponytail, and her strong eyebrows framed beautiful blue eyes. Her smile filled a room and lit up my soul. I'd see her after school when we were having basketball practice on one side of the gym while the women's team practiced on the other side.

Kirsten and I would see each other every day during practice. She'd catch me looking over at her and smile. One day I shot the ball and it bounced toward the other side of the gym. I could have jumped and snagged it, but instead I let it roll away. The trajectory was perfect. I waited a few seconds then ran over to the ball, which was now at Kirsten's feet. She kicked it up with her feet into her hands. She looked at me with her giant eyes and smiled.

Over the next few months we'd flirt and chat. We'd see each other in the hallway and make eyes at each other. Between walks home each day, we'd talk on the phone every night.

One night I tried telling my parents about Kirsten.

"Who are you talking on the phone with every night?"

"My friend."

"What's his name?"

"Her name is Kirsten."

"Oh, a girl!"

"Yeah."

"Is she Chinese?"

"No."

"Is she Asian?"

"No."

"Is she a Christian?"

"She grew up Catholic."

"So she's not a Christian."

"I gotta go."

Later that month, my parents announced that we were all getting dressed up and going to the Good Friday service at our church that night. I was sixteen and didn't want to go to a service in Cantonese on a weekend night. But my attendance was not optional.

Our church sanctuary was very David Lynch, lined with red pews and red carpet. The congregation started in with the hymns. I remember thinking, *I can't read these words. Ugh, I don't want to be here.*

Eventually I snuck out to use the bathroom. Afterward, instead of returning to the sanctuary, I veered into the dark church office and called Kirsten. We talked for an hour until the service ended and people started filing past the office. They couldn't see me, but I watched them walk out.

My older sister, Hannah, found me in the office. I was grounded for a month.

Like most Sevens, my process of becoming didn't fit. I was expected to be more Chinese, more academic, more fundamentalist, more of a rule follower.

I think about Nicodemus sneaking out to talk to Jesus at night (John 3:1-21). Being a part of the religious establishment at the time, he had to follow the rules of his religion and check its specific boxes. Anything outside those boxes was scandalous, including a rendezvous with the Son of Man. Nicodemus had followed the rules all his life. Jesus gave him a metaphor to save him. Imagine being born again . . . imagine being born into a life without the restrictions and repression of fundamentalism.

Take some time to reflect on what's being born in you (take a walk if possible) and consider the following:

- Imagine you are being birthed now. What are you being born out of? (What boxes and expectations are you shedding?)

- What are you being born into? (What expansive spaces can you now occupy?)

- What does it look like to more fully express who you are in this world?

CURIOUSLY JUDGING

SEVENS GET JUDGY UNDER STRESS.

I am world-class judgy. I am the Judge Judy of judging. I am so good at judging I can even judge myself judging myself. I am a postmodern meta judge.

My work of contemplation is to get my life and my spirituality out of my judgy head and into my body. My practice of contemplation involves three steps: noticing, practicing curiosity (without judgment), and then asking questions of meaning.

Recently I attended a contemplative retreat. The average age of the attendees was about fifty years old. The structure of the retreat involved teaching, ritual, and then practice. Rinse and repeat. Rituals help your body experience meaning by bypassing the judgment of the head. Through the course of the week all of the participants were supposed to volunteer for a ritual.

The last day came and the leaders asked, "Who has not yet volunteered? This is your ritual!" Four of us reluctantly raised our hands and went off to learn how the ritual would be conducted. It was beautifully dramatic and emotionally choreographed by a theater director.

Later that evening, we sat in a circle of fifty men. After a period of silence, we received our cue. No one else in the circle knew what was coming.

My three fellow volunteers and I rose in unison. Moving slowly, we met in the middle of the circle and then walked in step toward a water basin sitting in the middle of the room. Once we arrived at the pool of water, we slowly spread ourselves around it facing the circle of men watching us.

Next, we lifted carafes of water over our heads like Simba in *The Lion King*. We started to tilt the vessels until streams of water fell into the collective pool, then slowly lowered them as they emptied. I could feel the eyes staring at us. Dramatic classical music served as a backdrop. The entire scene represented the baptismal waters of life. It was a moving ritual.

As my carafe reached eye level, I noticed something odd about it. There was no stream of water coming out. I used my peripheral vision to glance at the other volunteers. There were only three streams being poured into the basin. My carafe was empty! I had forgotten to refill it after the last practice!

I stayed the course and continued to pour nothing out my carafe until it reached waist level. As we dramatically walked back to the center of the circle and then back to our seats, I sat down and experienced the full gamut of emotions.

First I felt embarrassed. I could feel the flush in my face intensifying. Then I felt anxious. I wondered if anyone had noticed. Had I ruined the ritual? Had the theater director seen me? He was probably disappointed in me. Then anger and shame took over, and my regular internal mantras of judgment started firing. The voices have been there since I was a young child.

What's wrong with me! Why am I so flighty?

Then I caught myself judging myself. *Why am I so hard on myself? Why am I so judgy?*

I took a deep breath and decided to try my contemplative practice. What did I notice? *I participated in a water ritual. After the practice I forgot to refill my carafe. I performed the ritual with an empty carafe.*

OK, so let's be curious about it. *Hmmm. What does this mean? Could this have a deeper meaning? What might this represent?*

It suddenly dawned on me. *Ohhhh, this represents my life. This is how I showed up to the contemplative retreat— on empty.*

I had poured and poured my life out without appropriate boundaries. My soul was bone-dry. The moment I made that connection, I felt seen by God.

A smile broke out on my face, and I started laughing.

Next time you're in a stressful situation, try the following:

- Take a deep breath.

- Notice what's happening, both externally and internally.

- Be curious about what's present. (Try not to judge.)

What questions come up about your experience?

THE NEW NEW

SEVENS COMPULSIVELY START THINGS. Since as an immigrant minority I didn't always belong, I developed a strategy to start communities I could belong to. I've started a family, two youth ministries, a college ministry, a collaborative art space, and a cycling club. I started my first community of belonging as a teenager on a basketball team.

Clement and I became friends while playing on rival high school basketball teams. We noticed that in Toronto, many high schools had at least one or two Asian kids on the team. We started talking about representation and bringing these Asian kids together to start a team. But what would we call the team? How could we culturally appropriate our own culture? How about . . . the Dragons?

We bought twenty navy blue T-shirts and ironed the word *Dragons* onto the front. On the back we ironed on numbers and our last names. Chu. Tsang. Chin. Lee. Names usually seen in math competitions and rarely seen on the back of a jersey. Over the next year we recruited the best Asian basketball players from around Toronto. We started winning games and then under-eighteen tournaments. People were confused. What? Where were these tall Asian kids from? *They can dunk?*

Many people say King Solomon was a type Seven. He integrated and asked God for wisdom to lead well. And he started many new projects. He was dazzled by shiny newness and didn't know when to stop. Perhaps it was overextension that led him to write the book of Ecclesiastes, which begins, "Meaningless! Meaningless! . . . Everything is meaningless" (Ecclesiastes 1:2).

As Sevens we need to remember that starting new things just to start new things is wind through our fingers. It is part of the gift of who we are—and at times it's an empty shadow.

Notice the movement in you to start new things.

Become curious about what starting a new thing moves you toward.

When you have an idea, pause and see if there is something you're wanting to move away from.

Find a good therapist to support you in being present with the things you want to distract yourself from.

CRYING MY WAY OUT OF MY HEAD

FOR FORTY-FIVE YEARS, I WAS pretty much emotionally blind. I thought my way through life. The way I understood feelings was through cognition.

"Wow, I bought three pairs of pants last week. Oh wait . . . I *think* I must have been sad! Crazy! Didn't even know. Hilarious!"

"Wait a minute, my stomach's been a mess for the last week. I *think* I must be pretty anxious and stressed. That's so interesting."

But life has a way of inviting you into yourself fully. Jesus calls this the narrow path (Matthew 7:14). You don't choose the narrow path. It comes knocking on your door, and everything inside you wants to run the other way—to join the masses on the wide road.

Last year my life fell apart and I cried my way out of my head. Buckets and buckets of tears. One morning I woke up weeping. I had never experienced that before. I awakened to consciousness and ugly crying. My first instinct was to make it go away. Grab my phone. Do some pushups. Take a shower. But I cycled through these distraction options and made a decision to stay in my sadness. For the next hour I cried. Decades of repressed sadness came flowing up.

I turned on a version of "Love More" and the faucet opened wider. My eyes poured out my life like a Wyoming waterfall. It was as if Moses' staff had tapped on me and God ordered the natural springs to start flooding. After another half-hour, the aquifer of my soul finally dried up.

I took a deep breath. I needed to get myself together since I had a wedding to officiate later that afternoon. A bike ride felt like a way to find my path back to sanity.

I pulled my road bike off the wall, filled my bottles, grabbed my helmet, and set out. Within minutes I was out of the city on quiet country roads. I fell into the quiet hum of the wheels spinning. My mind drifted from the grief I was experiencing, sorting through old memories like a photo album, to the present—being on my bike, the winter sun kissing my face, feeling like I was going to be OK. I rode back into the city. At home I hung up my bike, cleaned up, and made myself some food.

"How am I feeling?" I asked myself.

"I feel fine," I replied.

"Wait, fine's not a feeling."

"I feel hungry."

"Wait, also not a feeling."

"I feel grounded. I feel content and almost . . . happy?"

Nothing had changed. My grief was still present. It dawned on me that I had dived into my grief and touched the other side. But for most of my life, my Seven tendency to avoid sadness had kept me from fully living.

Later that week I told my therapist, Trish, about my morning of weeping. After patiently listening she asked, "So what are you feeling these days?"

I caught myself thinking and stopped. *OK, get into my body.* I wiggled my toes. Relaxed my shoulders. Closed my eyes and took a deep breath. What was I feeling?

"I feel . . . I'm feeling a lot. Honestly, these feelings seem paradoxical."

"Tell me more."

"I feel immense gratitude, in ways that are new and deeper, if that makes sense. *And* I'm feeling profound and sometimes overwhelming grief. I'm also feeling more grounded in myself than ever before *and* I feel wildly insecure. It's a lot. Sometimes I'd rather not feel, but I'm trying to feel my way through each day."

Trish smiled. It felt like her deep eyes were piercing into my soul. "Welcome," she said. "Welcome to your life."

Tears of gratitude flooded my soul, and one breached the walls of protection. It escaped out of my tear duct, down my cheek, and was set free into the world.

Narrow is the road that leads to life.

When emotions get overwhelming, how do you respond?

What life experience might be inviting you to get into your heart?

CEREBRAL CURSE

SEVENS HAVE A CEREBRAL CURSE. We spend our time in our heads and in the future. This often means entire segments of our day are occupied by lofty ideas, dreams, and plans for the future. For example, I am going to New York next week. I will spend this current week cerebrally in New York City even though physically I won't be there for another six days. The result of the cerebral curse is that present-day details are easily forgotten.

Ten years ago, we made plans to fly to Portland from Austin to see a favorite band of mine, Sigur Rós. We were traveling with friends who'd attended concerts with us before, and they knew I had a tendency to arrive at the venue without my tickets. Since we were flying across the country to see this show, every time we saw each other, our mantra was, "Don't forget your tickets!"

The day came to fly to Portland. We checked in, made it through the security line, and found our friends at the gate. "Gideon, do you have y'all's tickets?"

"I've got our tickets!"

"Good job! You did it!"

I was celebrated like a toddler who remembered to go potty.

For the next three days we hiked, biked, ate, and drank our way through Portland. Our last night was the highly anticipated Sigur Rós Concert. We took a nap at the Ace Hotel where we were staying and walked a mile to the venue through the cool, drizzly October night.

As we turned the corner, the lights of the marquee lit up the line of attendees like spotlights. In front of us in line was a woman with long black hair, bright red lipstick, and a gray wool trench coat. She was talking enthusiastically to her friend while waving her hands—which happened to be holding her tickets.

As I noticed the tickets, I reached into my jacket pocket and felt no tickets. A smile broke onto my face. My friends looked at me and immediately knew what that look meant. "No you didn't."

"Yes I did."

"No you did not . . . "

I turned and started running back to the hotel. The two-mile round trip warmed me up and I made it back halfway through the opening act. Jónsi was wonderful.

The one goal of the trip was not to forget the tickets. I still found a way to forget.

I recently read David's poem in the Psalms telling us to remember all of God's goodness.

For as high as the heavens are above the earth,
    so great is his love for those who fear him;
as far as the east is from the west,
    so far has he removed our transgressions from us.
    (Psalm 103:11-12)

Man, remembering isn't my strong suit. I've forgotten many, many things. I wonder what I've forgotten about all of God's goodness.

Start a goodness journal. Write down one memory of God's goodness each day.

LEARNING TO BE CELEBRATED

SINCE MY ARRIVAL, I've had an awkward relationship with my birthday. As a Seven I want the attention, yet once I receive the attention I can't handle it.

Not all Sevens may be like that, but my feelings are like a tide that advances and recedes. Love me! Get away from me! Do you love me?

Last February was my forty-sixth birthday, and I decided to practice sitting in the awkwardness and receiving the celebration of my friends. We went on a bike-camping trip to the high desert of Arizona. On my birthday we stayed the night in one of my favorite towns, Marfa, Texas. The next morning we drove to the Chinati Foundation, a large-scale-art gallery started by Donald Judd in the 1970s.

After an hour inside, I stood by the floor-to-ceiling glass wall gazing at the field outside. A roadrunner slowly walked up to me. Because of the glass he didn't know I was there. For several seconds I knelt and gazed into his eyes. I whispered, "Hey, Mr. Roadrunner. It's my birthday!" I swear he winked at me.

Later that night we arrived in El Paso and John began to prep a dinner of Brussels sprouts and steaks. I got up from my chair and asked if he needed any help. He looked at me and told me to sit down. "Hey, man, it's your birthday. I don't need your help. I'm making your birthday dinner." My instinct was to fight it, but I reminded myself to receive it.

With my belly full, I thanked John for the dinner and started to clean up the table. It was an unconscious action resulting from growing up in a transactional universe. I needed to earn any goodness that came my way. John looked at me and said, "Dude. Sit your ass down. It's your birthday. You ain't cleaning shit today. I'm glad you were born. I'm glad to do this." I sat back down with tears in my eyes.

Deep down, I realized that I didn't feel I was worthy of goodness or even kindness. There's a part of me that doesn't even fully believe I'm worth being celebrated on my birthday. I wonder if that's what Paul meant when he talked about "this love that surpasses knowledge—that you may be filled to the measure of all the fullness of God" (Ephesians 3:19). I wonder if we can offer that to each other and get a tiny glimpse of that fullness.

Do you feel like you are worthy of love and celebration?

How does it make you feel to hear that God wants you to know love that surpasses knowledge?

Who is someone in your life that can show you this love?

OPENING MY HEART

MY FRENCH BULLDOG LIKES EVERYONE. If Charles Manson walked into my house he'd run at him like he was Barack Obama. Similar to my Frenchie, Sevens also tend to like everyone. My theory is we're projecting our need to be liked onto them. Hopefully we'll get some likes back.

Thirteen years ago I spent a summer in Chicago finishing a seminary class to get the degree I'd started in the '90s. During my stint in Chicago I heard that Radiohead was coming to town the following week to play at the historic Chicago Theater. Tickets were predictably sold out. I hopped on Craigslist to see what was available: $800 for a pair, $900 for three tickets, $750 for a pair . . . I kept scrolling onto the second page and found one ticket available for $250. Hmmm. That seemed odd and under-priced. I sent the link an email.

A response came back immediately. "It's available!"

"Is it a physical ticket? How do I know this isn't a scam?" I wrote back.

"I'll meet you in person. In fact, let's grab dinner beforehand. I'll give you the ticket, and I'm actually going to the show too. I'll be sitting right next to you."

Like a French bulldog looking for a scratch on the neck, I agreed to this Craigslist blind date.

The next week came and I met my Craigslist date at a nice Italian restaurant across from the theater. We had a nice conversation over caprese salad and carbonara. Eventually, he asked what I did for a living. Usually I don't reveal that I'm a pastor until someone gets to know me. I told him I was a pastor.

"A pastor! Wow, that's crazy! I've never sat and had dinner with a pastor before! I can't upcharge you for your ticket!"

"It's fine. I don't mind. I agreed to it. In fact, you were the cheapest ticket on Craigslist."

We ended up agreeing that I would pay the face value of the ticket. Then we walked across the street to the show. For the next ninety minutes the flashing strobes, raspy voice of Thom Yorke, and intricate vibrations of Jonny Greenwood tickled my soul. After the show I started to say goodbye, and my new friend asked what I would be doing next.

"I think I might hit the bar across the street to watch the end of the game. I think LeBron's Heat are going to beat the Mavs tonight for the NBA championship."

"Mind if I come?" he responded.

So that evening I enjoyed a nice Italian dinner, got the best deal in town on a ticket, enjoyed a show, and watched the Heat win the NBA championship while sipping an old-fashioned *with a Craigslist stranger!* My heart was wide open, with the boundaries of a French bulldog.

Looking back I can see that if I couldn't say no to a stranger on Craigslist (who was a very nice guy, by the way), I wasn't saying the appropriate noes in my life and vocation. Because of the hurt I've experienced as a result of bad boundaries, my heart has slowly closed since that time.

My work as a Seven now is to reopen that heart, but with boundaries.

Once again King Solomon, the Seven of all Sevens, tells us, "Above all else, guard your heart, for everything you do flows from it" (Proverbs 4:23).

What does it look like to live an appropriately open-hearted life?

EXTREMELY ALIVE?

SEVENS GO TO EXTREMES TO FEEL ALIVE. I am inspired by the apostle Paul's description of his life: "I have been constantly on the move. I have been in danger from rivers, in danger from bandits, in danger from my fellow Jews, in danger from Gentiles; in danger in the city, in danger in the country, in danger at sea; and in danger from false believers" (2 Corinthians 11:26).

Once for vacation I traveled to Afghanistan. My friend was working for an NGO in Mazar-i-Sharif. I asked for an invitation to visit, which I needed in order to apply for a travel visa to enter the country.

A few good friends made the trip with me. On our last day we flew to Kabul to stay one night before catching our flight home the next morning. We decided to go to the bazaar to buy gifts for friends and family. Our host called a driver for us. We piled into a Toyota Corolla and drove past the gates of our compound, out into the streets of Kabul.

We passed three checkpoints without any problems. But at the fourth, our driver talked longer to the military personnel than he had on previous stops. Ten minutes passed and we started to get uncomfortable. One of my friends pulled out his cellphone to call our host. The military dude said a few words to the driver. The driver turned to us and said in English that he needed all of our passports and phones. We looked at each other, not knowing what to do. We sheepishly complied.

It's hard to explain the feeling of helplessness you get sitting in an intersection in an unfamiliar place, not understanding what the signs say or what people are saying to you, and giving up your documentation and phone. Twenty minutes passed. I could feel a large drop of sweat slowly drip its way down my back. I was getting more anxious by the minute. My stomach tightened up.

Another Corolla pulled up and a man walked up to our car. He pulled our driver out of the car and shoved him into the other vehicle. Our back door swung open. Two of my friends were pulled out and also placed in the other car. The last two friends and I were left behind, and we drove off into bumper-to-bumper traffic. We could see our friends two lanes from us. We looked out the window. We had no idea what was happening. At the time it 100 percent felt like we were being kidnapped.

It's a strange feeling when you get flooded. Internally there's so much adrenaline rushing through your body that your brain dissociates from what's happening, like you're watching a movie in slow motion. We lost sight of the other vehicle.

After forty minutes of traffic and panic, I whispered in my friend's ear to ask how much cash we had in case we needed to bribe them. We had $1,000 US between us.

We finally pulled into a government building. It felt like a relief. For the next six hours they kept us in separate jail cells, interrogated us separately, then gave our phones and passports back and sent us back to our guesthouse. One of my friends spent that night throwing up as his body processed the stress of our experience. It had been terrifying. I was exhilarated and felt alive.

That was my first trip to Afghanistan. I've since been back for more.

There have been times when I've romanticized the extreme lives of the women and men described in Scripture. Paul met great resistance in his mission to be a pioneer of Jesus' movement of love. To many, his stories of hardship sound like tragedy and sacrifice. Only a Seven can read about being beaten with rods, pelted with stones, and shipwrecked and experience FOMO.

Why do we Sevens need extreme experiences to feel alive?

What pain are we avoiding to get that drug-like adrenaline hit?

OPTIONS OF THE UNKNOWN

SEVENS ARE COMFORTABLE WITH a multitude of options. To many that feels paralyzing. To a Seven, it's more opportunities not to feel trapped.

A few years ago my older son, Joshua, was getting ready to graduate from high school. Being a Seven dad, I convinced him to take a gap year in Australia and Mexico, then go to college. However, he still needed to apply to college in his senior year.

We started looking at art schools. Our first visit was to Santa Fe. The photography professor looked like Bob Ross with a stylist. He had some good advice for a prospective art student: "If you want to join our fine arts program as a photographer, I can't guarantee you'll get a job," he told my son. "So if you want to make lots of money, think about it carefully. But if you want a good art education, this is a great place to be."

A few months later we went to St. Edward's University in downtown Austin. The campus is nestled on a hill near the iconic South Congress Avenue with its boutiques and restaurants. The buildings are stone with beautiful Spanish-tiled roofs. After the tour I turned to Joshua. "So what do you think?"

"Um, I don't know. Man, this feels so overwhelming. There are too many options. It feels like jumping into the unknown."

"You know that feeling you have right now, Joshua?"

"The overwhelmed feeling? Yeah. I want it to go away."

"That's actually what life feels like. Most of life is unknown. Once you survive the first decision to venture into the unknown, it gives you confidence to handle the next one. You're a smart kid and you make good decisions. You're going to do great."

I told him that two years ago. Last year, my own life shifted radically. For the first time since I was my son's age, I stand staring into the unknown beyond the horizon. I have no idea what I'll be doing, where I'll be living, or who I'll fall in love with. I have greater empathy for what Joshua was feeling. It's true. It's overwhelming. I'm trying to receive the very words I gave to my son.

I'm going to do great in the upcoming unknown. Think of all my options and possibilities!

What in your life feels unknown right now?

Where might God be in that invitation to step into the unknown?

What part of you as a Seven is excited and scared?

PATIENCE AND SUFFERING

SEVENS ARE IMPATIENT. Waiting is a discomfort we're unwilling to consent to. Several years ago my wife and I had both sets of parents in town for the holidays. We drove to San Antonio in two cars. After dinner, the plan was for me to line up a riverboat ride and let the rest of the crew know when to meet up again. I tapped my younger son, Noah, to come with me.

We found the line, which stretched four blocks down, spanned the bridge onto the other side of the river, then wrapped back around another three blocks.

"Are you kidding me?" my son asked. "We're going to get in this line?"

The week before I had spent some time with my brother-in-law, who teaches psychotherapy at a college in Southern California. We'd had a conversation about the difference between pain and suffering, and I passed on the insight to my son.

"Pain is just discomfort," I told him. "Suffering is your unwillingness to consent to the discomfort. If we consent to the discomfort of waiting, we'll lessen our suffering."

"What does that even mean?"

So, full disclosure: the night went swimmingly because I ended up bribing him with a video game he'd been wanting for a long time.

I was patient with Noah's impatience because I recognized a part of me in him. I threw fits as a kid when I had to wait. But the older I get, the more I learn that control isn't real. If I can truly consent to the discomfort, I can save myself a bit of suffering. Peter says patience in our suffering makes us strong, firm, and steadfast (1 Peter 5:10). I'm not there yet, but I'm willing to wait.

How do you react when your patience is tested?

What are you waiting for in your life right now?

What would it look like to consent to waiting for that thing?

HOPE AS A FUNCTION OF STRUGGLE

MY FIRST BIKE-CAMPING TRIP was a thirty-mile jaunt to a campground in the rolling hills of Austin's western suburbs. The west side of the city is scenic and filled with large mansions on cliffs with views of the Texas Hill Country. I live among the peasants in the floodplains.

It was a hot and muggy Friday night in July. When the temperature finally dropped below ninety degrees, my buddy Evan and I rode a few blocks over to my friend Lee's house. Lee owned a local bike shop called Eastside Pedal Pushers.

"This is going to be fun!" I proclaimed.

"Man, that's a lot of climbing," Evan mumbled.

"Why are we doing this in July again?" Lee asked, the voice of reason.

"I can't wait!" I said, blinded by positivity.

We set out on our '80s touring bikes carrying our sleeping bags and gear for the night. Traffic was heavy, so we took the gravel bike path along the water to head west. The sun was setting and we passed a few dog walkers and runners. After three hours of climbing and descending, we pulled into the parking lot for County Line, an old barbecue joint on the water. We were two miles away from the campsite.

"We did it!"

"Whew!"

"I'm starving. Like famine level. Like cannibal level almost."

We were sweaty and tired and ready to eat a cow. I really can't tell you how heavenly Texas barbecue tastes when you've been using your body and heart as the engine to climb hill after hill. Within minutes, the table looked like a cattle stall crime scene.

"Damn, I have no words for how heavenly that was."

"I can't move."

"I might throw up. I'm glad we're pretty much at the campsite. We've got two miles to go."

What we didn't know was that our last stretch was a mile up and a mile down. Instead of rolling slowly into the campsite, we embarked on one of the steepest climbs in Austin, averaging 15 percent gradients. We were on heavy touring bikes loaded with camping gear and had bursting stomachs.

"Take it easy," Lee said. "It's a long way to the top."

"Argh! Why!" Evan cried.

"We got this, baby! We can do this!" said my blind positivity.

The lactic acid started flooding my legs. I shifted into my small front ring. I could hear Evan and Lee breathing heavily behind me. I kept downshifting, hoping to make the pain go away.

"I don't think I can do this."

"I hate this."

"We got this, guy! One pedal at a time!"

After what felt like a torturous eternity, all three of us were almost to the top. The last thousand feet felt like ten miles. We each reached into our emergency bag of tricks. Evan got off his bike and started walking. Lee kicked into his granny gear, a front ring so small you could pedal wildly and barely move forward. He looked like a circus performer. I started traversing back and forth the entirety of City Park Road. Even though we were hurting, I started laughing.

"Guys, we're going the exact same speed!" I gasped amid my oxygen asphyxiation.

Evan, who was walking his bike, said, "I believe my solution might be the easiest."

Lee said nothing and continued to comically spin his pedals while barely moving.

And we got to the top. Threw our bikes to the ground.

"We did it!"

"Barely! I might throw up!"

Since that night I've thought about climbing that hill many times. Brené Brown says hope is a function of struggle. Each struggle we overcome gives us more hope for the next inevitable struggle. Paul says the same thing in these words: "We also glory in our sufferings, because we know that suffering produces perseverance; perseverance, character; and character, hope" (Romans 5:3-4).

What is a place of discomfort or struggle that you might be avoiding?

Try engaging that struggle as a practice of hope.

GLUTTONIZATION

GLUTTONY.

Gluttony, gluttony, gluttony. Sevens and our gluttony.

Here are all the ways I've gluttonized into the "more is better" way of living.

I once ate nine mangoes in one sitting. My mother needed help finishing them so I obliged. The first one tasted juicy and delicious. Honestly I don't remember the last four. I just remember seeing nine mango seeds and thinking to myself, *Maybe a bit much*. That night I was up all night with hives.

The only other time I had hives was after a crawfish boil. The fun of a crawfish boil is that you stand at a table and people keep dumping more crawfish onto it. I have no idea how many I ate. We started at noon and ended at 3:30. It was enough to give anyone hives.

In the last ten years I've owned more than fifteen bicycles. I know what you're thinking. You only have two legs! I'm like a catch-and-release fisherman, what can I say?

Two years ago I dragged my two teenagers around the country in a small Toyota camper for eight weeks. I learned many things. Eight weeks is too much time for a teenager to hang out with his parents. Also, after seven waterfalls in a day, you stop enjoying the waterfall. Maybe TLC had the same experience. Their advice from the '80s still rings true—don't go chasing waterfalls. After twelve waterfalls, I stopped.

Ten years ago, I took my staff on a trip to New York. Round trip tickets were thirty dollars. We opted not to find a place to sleep. We could eat our way through the city and camp out at the twenty-four-hour Apple store! Predictably, I was done eating after our fifth meal. I found myself wandering the East Village. I looked at my watch. It was 3 a.m. I was no longer having fun.

Before my fortieth birthday, I invited everyone I knew to my upcoming party, along with everyone I ran into over the course of a month. That night my house was packed, and I was filled with anxiety. I didn't want all those people there in my house. More was not better.

I think about Paul's advice in his first letter to a young Timothy: "Godliness with contentment is great gain" (1 Timothy 6:6). Maybe Paul was trying to say that when we connect with the image of God within us and are content with who we are, that's a beautiful way to engage life itself.

As I approach midlife, these are the small things I enjoy.

I love to walk my dog in the greenbelt in Austin. We can't walk far because his French bulldog face is genetically flawed. We walk a mile and he lies on his back in the middle of the street. It's his way of saying, "Enough."

I no longer seek out new restaurants. There's a Japanese restaurant named Kome near my house. I was sitting at the bar one night and an elderly white woman walked in, passed by the host, sat down at the bar, and opened a novel. No one spoke to her or asked her what she wanted. They simply brought out her food. She was a regular. From that night on I had a new life goal. I was going to go to the same restaurant and order the same thing each week until I could walk in and have someone bring me the same meal.

I am down to three bikes: a road bike, a gravel bike, and a mountain bike. I haven't bought a new bike in five years.

I like to sip one pour of whiskey in the evening.

Two slices of pizza are better than an entire pie.

The small and few things in life are more enjoyable to me than the treadmill of more. We can all learn a few things from our hives.

Do you tend to enjoy overdoing it?

What might you be trying to numb?

Make a list of things in your life that bring you true contentment.

WANNA HEAR SOMETHING FUNNY (SAD)?

SEVENS ARE ALLERGIC TO SADNESS like I'm allergic to the lactose in milk.

I grew up in a fundamentalist family that only celebrated positivity. "Why are you crying? Stop! Turn that frown upside down. Let's sing it together! 'I've got the joy, joy, joy, joy down in my heart.'"

Really? I don't feel any joy. I feel pretty sad actually. But OK, I guess I'm not supposed to feel that way . . .

Most of my life I've been drawn to sad people. They show me a beautiful side of reality that I didn't have access to growing up.

I have a friend who is also a Seven. One day she said, "Wanna hear something funny?" She proceeded to tell me how her ex had cheated on her with her best friend. She threw a glass of water into her best friend's face. I remember thinking, *That's not funny at all. It's a super sad, true love story.*

A few weeks ago my friend texted me. "How are things going with your quarantine life?"

I caught myself texting back, "Wanna hear a funny (sad) story?"

So this quarantine life is pretty funny (sad and hard). My son and I were in New York City the day the mayor shut down all public spaces, including all museums. I was touring Donald Judd's house in SoHo when the guide announced that we'd be the last group to visit. The next day we boarded a plane as we all continued to learn about COVID-19. I looked around at my fellow passengers from my middle seat near the back. No one was wearing a mask. I heard a cough two rows behind me. It was a pretty funny (scary and anxiety-filled) trip home.

The next two weeks were really funny too (sad and lonely). I loaded up on groceries and locked myself in my 800-square-foot house all alone. Each day was the same: I woke up, made myself breakfast, walked my dog, worked on my computer, made lunch, worked a bit more, ate dinner alone, listened to records, went to sleep. Rinse and repeat. For two weeks I had no human contact. I felt like I was being socially waterboarded. Pretty funny (lonely).

Yesterday I did a backyard hang with the same friend who had texted me a few weeks earlier. "How's quarantine life going?" my friend asked.

I was about to react with, "Fine" or "Pretty funny." But I closed my eyes and checked in with myself.

"Last week I thought I was getting the hang of it. I've been working with my therapist to get in touch with my anger. In fact, I started an anger journal. It was the first time in my life I've allowed some of my anger and rage to come out. Once that happened I dove headfirst into the deep end with an overwhelming wave of grief. I was in a tailspin for two weeks. So recently, my quarantine life has been deeply sad. It's been hard."

I noticed myself being honest about my emotions and felt deep compassion for myself. It wasn't funny at all. It was where I was at.

The Scriptures tell us to mourn with those who mourn and to weep with those who weep (Romans 12:15). For forty years I was so afraid of my sadness that I didn't know how to stand with those who were hurting. I'll spend the next forty learning how to complement my joy with sadness.

What part of your own sadness do you need to sit with today?

ANXIETY PERFORMERS

SEVENS ARE CHARMERS AND PERFORMERS. Some people have performance anxiety. Sevens have anxiety performance.

At the age of six I graduated to the rite of passage undertaken by every Chinese immigrant child: the Western classical instrument. Perhaps we can join the white elites via the white ivory! Let's tickle our way up the assimilation ladder!

I played the piano for twelve years. Every day was a struggle. Playing the piano was like eating vegetables or learning multiplication tables. Pure and utter discipline. I harassed my mother with complaints and sighs for four years.

One day at the end of a lesson my teacher handed me my books with a look of disappointment. I remember looking into her eyes and seeing her confusion. It's like she was asking, "Is Gideon *trying* to be that bad at the piano? Perhaps there's a medical condition that's stunting his musicality."

As I walked to the car with my mother, I sighed and muttered under my breath (as I had for the past four years), "I wish I could quit the piano."

My mother heard me and said, "Fine, you can quit."

"I *can*?"

"Yes, with one condition. You need to pick up another instrument."

Oooooh, the musical world was my fried oyster! What would I choose? The drums? I wanted Larry Mullen's flattop badly. This could be my chance! How about the saxophone? I could perm my hair and be a teenage Chinese Kenny G!

After a week of sleepless deliberation, I walked downstairs and declared, "Mother, I have decided which instrument I would like to invest my life in."

My entire family stopped and waited for my declaration. "Mother, I would like to be a student of the accordion."

That week my mother went through the yellow pages and found me an accordion teacher. For the next two years I took accordion lessons. I had accordion recitals!

One particular recital is etched into my memory. For some reason I was terrible at the piano but a god at the accordion. I awaited my turn to perform. Finally I was good at something! The room quieted when my turn came. With the stage lights bright in my face, I could barely see out into the dark auditorium. I closed my eyes and began to play.

I was on fire! I folded and unfolded like Michael Jordan on the basketball floor, like David Chang behind a fire, like Kusama painting a pumpkin. I could feel that the room was with me. I saw a tear trickle down the cheek of a woman in the front row. I decided to fully give myself to the song. I leaned forward and folded my accordion in. I leaned back with the unfold—only to realize that there was no back to the stool I was sitting on. There was a moment when I realized what was happening—my abs starting to shake as I tried to hold myself upright.

It was too late. I can still see it in slow motion: My abs finally relented and relaxed. The crowd gasped as I slowly fell off the stool and the weight of the accordion fell onto me like a typewriter. As I hit the ground the accordion finished unfolding like a sad Scottish funeral.

On that day my mother said, "Back to the piano it is." Six more years of vegetables. I was devastated.

It's been twenty-three years since I first got on stage to preach (perform) my first sermon. More than two decades of offering sermons to be loved. What would it look like for me to offer my presence and words out of love?

In the Scriptures, the word for "hypocrite" is also the word for "performer." You could say Jesus was upset with the religious leaders for not trusting that they were already loved. They had created a religious system to ensure that people performed for acceptance, even from God.

At a young age I was taught that life is a stage and our lovability has to do with our performance. As a Seven, that was my lane. I'd like to live in a different lane these days.

What are the ways we perform in life to earn love?

Who are the people you don't have to perform for?

What would it feel like to go through life like that?

HUMBLED TO BE EXALTED

SEVENS CAN PROJECT CONFIDENCE, so our insecurities come across as cocky. We're constantly measuring where we stand in the world. Who's behind me? Who's in front of me? For me, sports was a helpful measuring stick.

One day after school my son Noah wanted to shoot around at our neighborhood park. I wasn't planning to play but simply rebound the basketball. I was dressed in jeans, a casual shirt, and Blundstone boots. For about ten minutes Noah shot and I rebounded the ball back to him. My Achilles tendon felt safe.

While this was happening a young man in his twenties walked up to us. I didn't notice him until he was right behind me. "Excuse me, sir," he said.

I turned around and found I was eye level to his chest. I slowly looked up and made eye contact. He was at least six-three.

"Hey, guys, I'm Jeremy. Do you want to play twenty-one?"

I didn't, but as a Seven I couldn't say no.

In my head I kept reminding myself, *Go slow. Go slow. Don't get hurt.*

My son started the game off with a three-pointer. Jeremy backed me down in the post and easily laid it up over my head. He followed up with a jump shot. Noah crossed Jeremy over and drained a shot back at the corner of the free throw line.

"What's the score?"

"Noah's got two, Jeremy's got two, Gideon hasn't scored yet."

My competitive juices kicked in and I forgot that my Achilles and hamstring were ripe for the pulling. Jeremy backed me down in the post again. All my tricks from years of playing against bigger competitors came back to me. I got low to stabilize and put a forearm into his back to prevent him from backing me up. I knew he was going to back hard to get closer. The instant I felt the hard push, I let go and he stumbled backwards, catching himself from falling. I grinned. This move was called pulling the chair. As he stumbled I stole the basketball and dribbled to the top of the key. My son started laughing. He hadn't seen that wily veteran move before.

"Nice one, Dad."

Jeremy was slightly embarrassed, so he rushed up to the top of the key to guard me. I wasn't sure I still had the quickness to take advantage of my speed. I rocked the ball back and forth between my legs. I dribbled to my right and Jeremy came with me. I hesitated and crossed to my left. Once I got my hip past him I knew I had the bucket. I took three quick steps and could feel Jeremy closing behind me. I slowed down to feel him on my back. I took two more quick steps and laid the ball up on the first step with my left hand. Jeremy bit and tried to block my shot. I brought the ball back down, rocked it to my right hand to the other side of the basket, and laid it in.

Noah jumped up in the air. "Dad, that was *wet*!"

I wasn't sure what that meant but I took it as a compliment.

I scored the next twenty points trying to impress my son. Bucket. Game. I was dripping sweat down my shirt. My jeans were stuck to my legs. I was not in basketball shape. I tried to control my breathing so it didn't look like I was about to have a heart attack.

Jeremy grabbed the ball as it fell through the basket. He slammed the ball down on the court. "Let's run it back!"

Noah came and gave me a high-five. "Dad, that was sick." He could see the hesitation on my face when it came to playing a second game. "I can play with him if you want to take a break."

"I'm good, son. Let's go."

They gave me the ball at the top of the key to start since I'd won the last game. I checked it to Jeremy; he threw it back to me and slapped the ground to play defense. I dribbled into the lane and did a jump-shot with two feet and a dramatic head fake.

I felt a pop in my left leg. Instead of putting the ball up, I let go of it and limped off the court. I knew immediately I had pulled a hamstring. "I'm done, you guys. Go ahead and finish the game."

I tried to walk it off. I'd done it. The thing I didn't want to do. But I got my son's approval. It was worth it. I upped myself two levels, and then my hamstring brought me back down to earth.

The Scriptures talk about how those who exalt themselves will be humbled and those who humble themselves will be exalted (Matthew 23:12). My aging body is constantly finding a way to humble me. Richard Rohr says he tries to get humiliated at least once a day. That way he knows who's running the show—his ego or his true self.

When was the last time you were trying to impress but got embarrassed instead?

How does it feel when you get embarrassed?

DO I WANNA HANG
OUT THOUGH?

I HAVE A FELLOW SEVEN FRIEND named Keith. He's one of the few male Sevens I enjoy hanging out with. We met on Flickr back when Flickr was Instagram. We admired each other's photography.

Years later I decided to get my first tattoo. I was drawn to more minimalist modern designs. I messaged Keith and we met up.

"Hey, man, I've loved your photography for a while," I told him.

"Thanks, man. You too."

"So I'm thinking about a tattoo. I know you're a graphic designer. I dig your minimal style. It's right up my aesthetic preference."

"Oh wow, thanks, man. What an honor to hear that."

"So I'm thinking of getting a tattoo on my left arm. I want something like a family crest based on our Chinese zodiac."

"I love that idea. What are your zodiacs?"

"I'm a tiger, my wife and my older son are rabbits, and my younger son is a monkey."

"Damn, a tiger, two rabbits, and a monkey. I'd be super psyched to design something like that. Count me in!"

We talked for another twenty minutes. As we were leaving Keith turned to me.

"Man, I really feel like we connect at a deep level. We should be friends, man. Let's hang out sometime!"

"Yeah, I'd love to hang out."

"Let's do it soon!"

"Deal."

"All right, love you man. See you soon."

Did he just tell me he loved me? I think he did, and we'd just met.

The next Sunday our liturgy was winding down at the end of the service. We sang the last song, Naomi gave a beautiful benediction, and, as we did every week, we sent our congregation out with these words: "Go live as the church, and see you throughout the week."

I made small talk with the people around me. Out of the corner of my eye I noticed a person walking quickly and deliberately toward me. Before I could finish my conversation, I felt a tap on my shoulder. I turned toward my interrupter.

"Hi, I'm Chad," he said. "This is my first time here."

"Hey there, how's it going? I'm Gideon. Nice to meet you, Chad. Where are you from?"

"I've lived in Austin for ten years now. I've been at five churches, and the last one I couldn't handle theologically. What's your theology?"

This question from visitors is a red flag. It means they're looking for a certain set of cognitive boxes to check before they engage with us. They're usually a poor fit for our community.

"Well, you know, theology is a big subject. For us it's more about mystery than certainty."

"What's your view on atonement and eschatology?"

I've been to seminary and I know what these words mean. However, I've also been pastoring long enough to recognize their weaponization. I knew immediately that this person wasn't going to be a good fit with us. How could I get out of this conversation?

"It was nice to meet you. I'm sorry, but I have a lunch meeting I need to get going to."

"Maybe I'll email you some questions."

"Yeah, uh, sure."

"What's your email?"

"Go ahead and email info@voxveniae.com."

"Do you have a personal email?"

"I do, but I don't always give it out. Again, glad you were able to visit. Have a great Sunday and let's hang out sometime!"

I walked away and those words rang through my head. Why did I say that? I clearly did not want to hang out with him. Why was that my go-to to get out of a conversation? Did I want people to like me so badly that even my rejections felt like invitations? What would be the kinder thing to say?

I think about Jesus' life. He was kind enough to be present to each person where they were at. He was able to love because he didn't need everyone to be his friend. He could be honest with the woman at the well in Samaria and bless her with hard truth (see John 4:1-26). He could invite himself over to Zacchaeus's house as a friend but also to confront his greed (Luke 19:1-9). He probably didn't make too many buddies turning over tables in the temple (Mark 11:15-18). He had a higher value than being liked: it was simply to love.

What do you do to be liked?

What would it look like to be loving even when it's hard?

FOLLOWING ALIVENESS

ONE OF THE THINGS I ENJOY about being a Seven is the capacity to follow what makes me alive—to allow myself to enjoy the fullness of doing what I truly love. It often surprises me how seldom people are willing to do what they love.

My son and I traveled to New York City recently. Joshua was in his freshman year of art school in Denton, and he had never been to New York as an adult. I wanted to show him around and go museum hopping. As a Seven I love tailoring adventures to the people I care about. I find a lot of joy in creating experiences of joy. So I created an itinerary that would make most people want to nap just reading it.

On our last day we enjoyed a delightful meal at a Greek restaurant. With lamb and red wine in our bellies we set out to return to our hotel. As we were walking, Joshua asked me, "What do you think this season of your life is going to be like?"

"You know, I'm a pretty simple person," I answered. "I have a few things I love and I kind of know what I'm into."

"What are you into?"

"It's probably just cycling, art, and spirituality."

"That's true. I wonder if I'll find my few things."

"Totally you will. It's nice when you figure yourself out. You know, actually, I'm also into traveling."

"You're right. You do love to travel. It's one of your favorite things in life."

"And I'm into books, too. I love to read."

"OK, so cycling, art, spirituality, traveling, reading. You're up to five."

"Yeah, so I have five."

A few minutes passed as we walked in silence. The sounds of New York served as our background music: sirens, voices in conversation, car alarms.

"I might add one more. I don't pretend to be well-versed in films or the history of cinema, but I do love a good art-house film."

"OK, so now you're adding movies."

"Oh, I thought of another one. Photography."

"Yeah, you definitely can't forget photography. You might want to move that up higher on your list."

"And also I love psychology and sociology. And theology. Don't forget theology. I love theology. And contemplation. Also contemplation."

"OK, so you're not that simple. You actually have more passions than most people I know."

Jesus talks about how he came to earth to help us live a full life (John 10:10). I'm learning that "more" doesn't always mean "full." I'm interested in many things. But I'm starting to choose fewer so that I can enjoy more.

What are the few things in life that fill your cup? What do you love to do?

How can you spend your time doing less but more of what you truly love?

SHAME PROTECTOR

AS A SEVEN, I FIND THAT MY ANXIETY is my protector from shame.

A few weeks ago I stopped by my neighborhood coffee shop for an afternoon treat. Flat Track is connected to a bike shop, and since I'm pretty connected to the cycling community in Austin, I often run into acquaintances there. My move is usually to get a coffee to go and then wave and bounce. I'll do anything to avoid unnecessary small talk.

But on this day I had an hour to kill between appointments, and I was out of coffee beans at home. I decided to get some beans and to treat myself to an oat cortado. I walked up to the counter where my friend Cassie, who manages the place, was working that day. I gave her a high-five.

"How's your day comin'?" I asked.

"Ugh. Too long. Almost done, though."

"Cool, hang in there."

"Do you want anything with your bag of beans?"

"I'll take an oat cortado, please."

"Sounds good. With your discount, that'll be fourteen dollars."

I paid, grabbed my bag of beans, and walked around the counter to wait for my drink. I noticed two cycling acquaintances sitting at the bar nearby. I was too close to pretend I hadn't seen them.

Aaron looked up, smiled, and gave me a nod. I walked over with arms open and said, "Hey, Aaron! Good to see you."

We hugged. Next to him was his partner. I'd met her several times and had held a number of conversations with her. I should know her name. Since I'd hugged Aaron, I went for a side hug with her.

"Hey, Vanessa!"

She didn't move or respond because her name was not Vanessa. She was facing the other way. My attempt at a side hug felt like a tap on her shoulder. She turned to face me and I ended up giving her an awkward neck hug.

"What did you say?"

"I said hi, . . . "

"What's my name, Gideon?"

"Your name is Va—"

"Veronica."

"Yes! Veronica!"

Aaron and Veronica started laughing. All the blood rushed to my face.

"Um, Cassie, could I get that oat cortado to go, please?"

I walked to my van. Immediately I went to shame. *Ugh, what's wrong with me? Why did I do that? Argh, so embarrassing. Why can't I remember anyone's name?*

In the scheme of things, I simply made a mistake. But I noticed how quickly I went from "I made a mistake" to "I *am* the mistake."

That interaction happened three weeks ago. I am 100 percent positive that Veronica hasn't thought about it once. I've thought about it twice a week for three weeks.

Sometimes I wonder about the origin of my shame. And I've come to realize that a lot of my anxiety is to prevent me from feeling the weight of shame in my life. For me, faith is to trust that even though that's how I see myself, that's not how God sees me.

In *Tattoos on the Heart*, Gregory Boyle writes, "The God, who is greater than God, has only one thing on Her mind, and that is to drop, endlessly, rose petals on our heads. Behold the One who can't take His eyes off of you. Marinate in the vastness of that."

Could it be true that I am a flawed human who makes mistakes *and* God fully sees me and not only loves me but likes me? It takes great faith to trust the vastness of that kind of love.

How do you respond when you make a mistake?

How long does it take to go from "I made a mistake" to "I am the mistake"?

How does it feel to know that you're flawed and fully loved and liked?

SOCIAL ANXIETY
EXPERIMENTS

THE ENNEAGRAM HELPED ME befriend my anxiety. If you
had asked me before I encountered the Enneagram if I was
an anxious person, I would have said no, I'm a fun person.
If you'd asked me if I had social anxiety, I would have said
no, I'm an extrovert and I love making friends.

A few years ago I flew up to Seattle to speak at Inhabit, a
conference for people engaged in spiritual communities and
activism. I was invited to attend a pre-party the night before
for speakers. We met in the basement of Fremont Abbey, a
beautiful old church turned into an event space in Seattle.

I arrived in the city and borrowed a bike from my friend. I
ate a quick dinner and biked over to Fremont from Capitol
Hill. The abbey was at the top of a long hill. By the time I arrived I was covered in drizzle and sweat. I walked around the
neighborhood to turn the faucet of sweat off and cool down.

As I walked toward the building for the party I decided
to check in with my emotions. What was I feeling right now?
Sweaty.

OK, not an emotion.

Heartburn.

Also not an emotion.

OK, actually, anxiety.

What did I have anxiety about?

I would probably know just a few people in the room—maybe four people out of seventy-five. Would those four people be there? Would I have to make small talk with strangers?

Ahhh. The anxiety started to make sense.

So what do I usually do to soothe my anxiety at parties? Grab a beer, find someone I know, and start talking to them. I wondered what would happen if I didn't talk to anyone. I could grab a drink, sit in the room, and wait for someone to talk to me. I could leave my phone in my pocket.

Whoa. That was crazy and scary. I wanted to try it.

I took a deep breath, opened the door to the basement event space, and walked in. The room was buzzing. It was already wall-to-wall people. Everyone had either a drink or a plate in their hands. Small groups were scattered all over the place. The sounds of conversation and laughter combined to create the familiar hum of a party. A live band was playing in the background.

As my eyes adjusted to the dark room, I instinctively started scanning for familiar faces. I saw Tim in one corner and Paul sitting next to his partner, Liz. On the far side of the room was Dwight. I noticed how naturally that came to me. I was like a social bounty hunter. OK, stick to the plan.

I walked in, got in line at the bar, and waited. I could feel my anxiety rising. *Pull out your phone! Pull out your phone!* I pulled my phone out of my rear pocket to Xanax my anxiety, but then I stuck to the plan. I put it back in the other pocket. I noticed the shortness in my breathing. *Breathe, Gideon. Breathe.* The five-minute line to get my drink felt like five hours.

"What would you like to drink, sir? We have red wine, IPA, and a cider."

"I'll take wine, please."

I put a few dollars in the tip jar and started walking in Tim's direction. But then I remembered the plan. I saw an empty table in the middle of the room. I sat down.

What was I feeling right now?

A whole lot of anxiety.

Man, the phone would be super helpful. I took a large gulp of the red wine. I again noticed my shallow breathing. I took in a long, deep breath, but the anxiety only rose. It was almost like a force was trying to push me out of my seat and make me walk over to the person next to me to start a conversation.

I scanned the room. Was I being super awkward? Was everyone wondering why this weirdo was sitting by himself?

Be present, Gideon. What do you see around the room? I saw a man with thinning white hair and a moustache. He had a safari vest on. What an interesting fashion decision. He was talking to a woman wearing a large hat.

I wondered how much of my buzz was fueled by social anxiety.

I wondered what percentage of people in this room were present and fully enjoying themselves.

Did people actually like small talk?

How many people were trying to end their conversations?

I sat there for the longest ten minutes of my life. I started sweating. *Oh, wow, my anxiety is producing a reaction in my body. This is truly fascinating and utterly terrible to experience. Do introverts feel like this?*

Finally, Cassie saw me from across the room. She tapped on my shoulder and relieved me of my own tortuous experiment. It felt like I'd been holding my breath like a free diver and had finally come up for air.

I think of Jesus' words in Matthew about his yoke being easy and his burden being light (Matthew 11:30). I wonder if he had seen an ox that morning laboring under a heavy yoke. I wonder if he could see with deep empathy the weight of our need to be loved and how that affected our day-to-day lives. If we knew how much we were truly loved, wouldn't each day, each task, each moment be lighter? How much of the burden that I carry each day is my social anxiety?

How heavily do people's opinions of you weigh on you each day?

Why do you need to be liked?

LIMINAL RESISTANCE

RECENTLY I WENT BIKE CAMPING WITH TWO FRIENDS. In Texas we camp in the fall—summer camping is a feat of endurance and discomfort reserved for the strong and/or dumb. Our plan was to bike fifty miles to a campsite and arrive back home on Thanksgiving Day.

I got my green Rivendell Hunqapillar set up with a rear saddlebag and handlebar bag and tied my sleeping bag and pad down on the front fork.

As I loaded up my bike, I had a decision to make: Should I pack my hammock or my tent? I checked the weather app on my phone, which showed a low of fifty overnight. Hammock it was.

The next morning I checked my gear, turned on my lights, and rode out into the dark to meet my friends at a coffee shop downtown. I wove my way through familiar neighborhoods as the sun started to peek from behind the houses. I crossed the bridge, turned left, and saw the café in the distance. As I neared I saw Nick and Josh waving at me. I rang my bell and waved back.

The sun burst into the sky and we rode fifty glorious miles to Krause Springs outside of Austin. The summer swimming crowd was absent and the landscape was glowing with autumn oranges and reds.

After cooking some sausages over a fire, finishing a bottle of wine, and sipping some whiskey, we called it a night. I laid out my sleeping bag in the hammock and climbed in, quickly falling asleep to its gentle rocking. The temperature was perfect.

A few hours later a surprise cold front blew in. I was awakened by twenty-mile-an-hour northerly winds. My toes and nose got colder and colder. Through my eyelids I could tell it was still dark—way too early to wake up. I tried to shush my brain to sleep. *Shhhh . . . Shhhh . . . It's OK, it's sleepy time.* After forty-five minutes of restlessness, I gave up, opened my eyes, and checked my phone: 2 a.m.

It felt like I was awake for the next four hours. I probably did sleep some, but I was in that in-between state of sleeping and waking. I'm sure you've had nights like that. Emotionally it was torture. I had no control and no way to change my situation; I could only wait. Those in-between states are the worst.

Theologians have a word for seasons of life that feel like that. They call it "liminal space." It's when life takes control away from us and forces us to live in the desolate present with no answers for the future. Examples of things that thrust us into liminal space include loss of a loved one, a move, a change in beliefs, loss of friendship or identity, a child leaving home, being rejected, and so on.

Richard Rohr describes this space as one of the most important for spiritual transformation. In a meditation on the Center for Action and Contemplation website (cac.org), he writes:

> We have to allow ourselves to be drawn out of "business as usual" and remain patiently on the "threshold" (limen, in Latin) where we are betwixt and between the familiar and the completely unknown. There alone is our old world left behind, while we are not yet sure of the new existence. That's a good space where genuine newness can begin. Get there often and stay as long as you can by whatever means possible. It's the realm where God can best get at us because our false certitudes are finally out of the way. This is the sacred space where the old world is able to fall apart, and a bigger world is revealed.

I've spent all of 2019 and 2020 so far in liminal space. I don't like it. I'm trusting that this is a season of growth outside of my control. I wish I could tell you I understand all the lessons and why they are happening. Perhaps one day I will. In the meantime, feel free to join me in a mini loss-of-control tantrum.

What part of your life might be in liminal space right now?

How does the lack of control make you feel?

REFRAMING

SEVENS KEEP THEIR WORLD POSITIVE BY REFRAMING.

In the twelfth year in the life of the church I pastor, we purchased a building three blocks from the abandoned bar we had called home for more than a decade. The renovation process was exciting. I curated several artists from our community to paint art on our walls with quotes that represent our values.

When you walk in the front door you'll see, "Todos son bienvenidos" ("All are welcome"). Inside the foyer is, "Welcome, welcome, welcome," taken from Thomas Keating's prayer. As you walk into the sanctuary, the space above the door reads, "Love is her name." Inside the sanctuary on the back wall it says, "I am what I am."

That's right. In our brand new building, stenciled in large letters for all to see, in God's words to Moses—perhaps one of the most profound statements in all of Scripture—is a typo. It should have said, "I am who I am" from Exodus 3:14.

Since it was too much work to repaint and re-stencil this massive typo, I went into full-on Seven reframing mode. Embarrassingly, I even included it in a homily.

This is what I argued. Is it possible that "I am what I am" is more theologically correct than "I am who I am"? The Franciscans talk about how the universe is God's first incarnation. Not only are humans sons and daughters of God, but so is all of creation. We are brothers and sisters with beluga whales, El Capitan, the Himalayas, and all of existence. Then I went so far as to give the literal Hebrew translation, which is, "I will be what I will be."

I ended my homily with a live informal poll of the congregation. And guess what? It worked! More people now preferred my explanation of "I am what I am." Reframing complete.

I felt a mix of both relief and shame. I could have just apologized and owned up to my mistake. And I could have simply paid the artists to correct the mistake.

When was the last time you made a mistake?

Do you find yourself reframing in order to avoid taking responsibility?

GO WITH THE . . . FLOW?

I OFTEN HEAR WISDOM TEACHERS talk about going with the flow. We meditate in order to consent to the flow of God in our lives.

I'm not sure I know what that means. It sounds like it might limit my options. Are Sevens able to go with the flow? Depends on what the flow is, I guess.

My friend Robert grew up in Austin. He's a knowledgeable environmentalist and bona fide thrill seeker. One day after liturgy he walked up to me and said, "I've been tracking the water levels in Barton Springs. It's one of the few times a year that we can go whitewater rafting in it."

"Really? *The* Barton Springs that's in your backyard?"

"That's the one. You down?"

"Hell, yeah!"

The next morning my friends Jason, Claudia, and Nathan and I showed up at Robert's house. We loaded up six inflatable kayaks, oars, life jackets, and helmets into his Jeep Grand Cherokee.

After winding through Austin's morning traffic, we dropped into a canyon past the mansions of West Austin. We unloaded the gear and started inflating the rafts.

Our starting point was underneath the concrete structures of Highway 360. Robert gave us a quick safety demonstration, explained that we'd be floating across six sections of rapids, and demonstrated how to point our feet when we fell out of the kayak.

"When you tip over, point your feet downstream and go with the flow."

I got into the kayak first and took my seat, then Jason hopped in. We put two paddles in the water, ran straight into the concrete pillar, and tipped over. Corrie, Robert, Nathan, and Claudia laughed and applauded.

For the next four hours it felt like we were in a wilderness canyon. We were actually floating down the middle of our city.

After fifteen minutes of paddling we came upon our first rapids, which ended with a waterfall. We knew the waterfall was just a couple of feet tall, but it still looked intimidating to see rushing water drop off out of view. We had to traverse around a few bushes. The goal was to hit the waterfall straight on. Jason did a masterful job steering us. We dodged the bushes, he hit me in the head a couple times with his oar, then he pointed the kayak toward the waterfall.

"Let's go with the flow, baby!"

"We're going with the flow!"

What is the flow of life that you're in right now?

What part of the flow are you trying to resist?

OVERLY PRODUCTIVE ANXIETY

IT TAKES SOMEONE YOUNG AND DUMB to look at an institution that's been around for a few centuries and think, *I'm going to fix all of the problems the church has accumulated over the years.*

But in 2006 that's what I set out to do. I was thirty-two years old and, with a group of Chinese college students, started a church in the urban center of Austin. We called it the Voice of Grace. (Pretty arrogant name in hindsight. Look out, Austin! We've got grace and you don't. We're comin' your way!)

There was a lot of anxiety involved in starting a church. Who would come? Could we afford to stay open until the next weekend? Would people keep attending? Were we re-creating the problems of the institution? Were we innovating change at all?

As a Seven, I start new things to appease my anxiety. It's a poor strategy. I thought, *Starting a church is so stressful. What should I do? I know! Let's create an intentional community.*

Within a year we had purchased five homes within a quarter mile of each other. Sixteen of us moved in. I hired my friend Kevin, who had just graduated from seminary, to run the homes. But instead of appeasing my church plant anxiety, the situation quickly turned to chaos. We had to deal with a newly married couple facing mental illness. Roommate misunderstandings abounded. A bipolar stalker threatened the safety of our women. This intentional community was intensifying my anxiety!

Now what could I do to ease the anxiety? *I know! Let's take over an abandoned bar and turn it into a community center!*

I was biking home one day from downtown and passed a one-story abandoned, white building. There was a sign nailed onto the boarded-up windows. I called the number.

Chesters had been a BYOB club. Its front door opened into a tiny foyer where the cover fee was paid. The next set of doors revealed a dark room with a blue ceiling so low I could touch it on tippy-toes. On the molded carpet there were needles, condoms, vodka bottles, and cockroaches. All the amenities you would want in a church building. Somehow we decided this place would be a great spot to create community.

I now was in charge of a new church, an intentional community, and a community center. It was a nice cocktail for burnout.

In Matthew 6:25-34, Jesus tells us to look at birds and flowers. They don't worry about what they wear or what they'll eat next. Why is it so hard for us to trust that our needs will be met? Why do we create more anxiety in our attempts to appease our anxiety?

Are you able to notice your anxiety?

What's the relationship between starting new projects and your anxiety?

UGH . . . TITLES

SEVENS DON'T LIKE TITLES. Titles are an obstacle to freedom.

In my twenty years of being a pastor, I've never had a business card. "I'm so much more than a pastor!" I say to no one who's listening. "I'm an artist, a writer, a photographer, a cyclist, a public speaker."

My neighborhood liquor store is owned by a boisterous woman named Kiki. We have a three-year relationship based on Japanese whiskey. Despite the many conversations we've had, she has no clue what I do. The word "pastor" never comes up. Recently I stopped by to pick up a bottle of chianti on my way to a dinner party. One of my parishioners was in the store. We made eye contact and her eyes lit up with recognition. As we hugged, she yelled out, "This is my pastor! I go to his church across the street!" She pointed out the window. You could see the corner of our building two blocks away. I sheepishly shrugged, bought my bottle of wine, and snuck out the door. I couldn't believe she'd outed me.

Why was I embarrassed? There are several possibilities.

First, a pastor in the antireligious climate of Austin, Texas, has a social standing barely higher than a pedophile. If I ever want to end a conversation, I tell people, with lots of uncomfortable eye contact, "Hi there. I'm a pastor." They always walk away.

Second, the Scripture writers talk about our need to live a life worthy of the calling we've received (Ephesians 4:1). I have a complicated relationship to the idea of a calling. Are we called for life or perhaps for different seasons? How is my calling different or the same as my vocation and work? Why am I uncomfortable with the title of my calling?

Third, Sevens don't like to get pinned down to a title for fear of having to be accountable to other people's expectations of that label. We are often lauded for being the jack of all trades. Turns out that can be a clever strategy to evade and slip through life's responsibilities.

Hi, my name is Gideon Tsang, and I am a . . . (gulp) pastor.

As Sevens, why is it difficult to own the calling we've been given?

How do we avoid the responsibility of being who we actually are?

PERMIT TO LEARN

SEVENS ARE QUICK LEARNERS.

When I was thirteen, my sixteen-year-old friend taught me how to drive his parents' Toyota Celica with a manual transmission. I remember the feeling of revving the engine. I can still feel the cold steering wheel in my hand. It was exhilarating being in full control of this metal machine. I can still picture myself letting go of the clutch for the first time and feeling the machine move across the road. It was breathtaking. After a few weeks I had mastered the clutch and drove effortlessly around our hilly neighborhood. I was thirteen and my voice hadn't changed yet.

In Alberta, Canada, in the 1980s you could get your learner's permit at fourteen. After my birthday, my dad set up a day for me to learn how to drive. We had a first-generation green Honda Civic with a beige interior.

"Gideon, are you ready for your first driving lesson?"

"I sure am!"

"I want to teach you to drive a manual transmission car. That way if you're ever stuck or a war breaks out, you can drive any car on the road."

(Immigrants always base their decisions on future projections of worst-case scenarios. Usually a good ol' war.)

"Sounds good, Dad."

My dad pulled the car out of the garage and backed it into the street.

"OK, Gideon, why don't you get into the driver's seat?"

"Got it."

"Now the clutch is the tricky part. It controls your shifting and how fast you start the car. Why don't you keep the handbrake up? Push the clutch down to get a feel for the gearbox. Shift it into first. Don't let the clutch go or the car will lurch forward and stall. OK, good. Now try second gear, third, fourth, fifth, and reverse. Good job!"

"Thanks, Dad."

"Now let's try driving. Be careful, OK? Let the clutch up slowly as you give it some gas. Nice and easy."

I pushed down the clutch, put it into first, and effortlessly balanced the clutch and gas as the car moved forward—just as I had been practicing for the last three months. I shifted into second, signaled right, and pulled out of our cul-de-sac. My father was in shock.

"Wow, son! You are a naturally gifted driver! Good job!"

"Thanks, Dad."

I drove around our neighborhood for the next thirty minutes without stalling. I even pulled onto a hill to show off my ability to suspend the car on an incline using just the clutch. I could tell my father was both confused and proud.

My appetite for speedy learning shifted to new ideas as I entered the world of books and theology. I found myself giving a hearty "yes" to passages of Scripture like, "Anyone who belongs to Christ has become a new person. The old life is gone; a new life has begun!" (2 Corinthians 5:17 NLT). This means we're constantly becoming new! Uh, yeah!

In another letter, Paul invites us to "be transformed by the renewing of your mind" (Romans 12:2). This also has the flavor of constant renewal and ongoing transformation.

The capacity of the Seven for new experiences, foods, people, thoughts, and so on is part of what makes us sparkle for others. It is part of our gift and also at times casts a shadow of avoidance over what we already know. Most of us have enough knowledge or wisdom for ten lifetimes. Our challenge is to live deeply into fewer things.

How do you experience your appetite for learning?

Are the things you're interested in transforming you in a meaningful way?

Are you using learning to avoid something present in your life?

IDEOLOGICALLY
CAFFEINATED

WE SEVENS OFTEN FIND OUR IDENTITY in our ability to think quickly. I recently understood this via my love for coffee.

I love everything about coffee. I love the smell. I love the look of the beans. I love the morning preparation routine. I love the packaging and typeface of my preferred Flat Track bean. I love the *ping* of the beans hitting the container on my coffee scale. I love the *clink* of the ceramic dripper being placed onto my mug. I love the way the grounds foam and bubble as I drizzle boiling water onto them. I love the slow drip into the mug, the smell of heaven rising, and that first dark, nutty, slightly bitter taste on my tongue. *Ugh*, I love coffee so much.

Last Lenten season, I decided to give up caffeine for forty days.

The morning after Ash Wednesday I woke up, put on some hot water, and opened my bag of beans. Oh, wait. That's right. No coffee. I poured myself a glass of water and sat on my front porch. Just wasn't the same. The next few days I walked around in a fog with my head pounding. Each moment felt hazy, and I hated how sluggish I felt. It took me longer to answer questions. Writing an email was a struggle. It felt like all my superpowers had been taken away.

When I was in seventh grade our family moved to Hong Kong for my father's work. It was a difficult yet formative time for me. Growing up as a minority in Canada, I had thought moving to Hong Kong would finally take me out of the margins. Instead I was even more marginalized. I looked like the people I went to school with, but culturally I was still across the ocean. In addition to the social challenges, I went from being a straight-A student who skipped a grade in math to being painfully behind. School was now overwhelming. My grades plummeted and I was shamed for it. For the next five years I stopped trying academically. The message I received from my family was that I wasn't a hard worker or intelligent.

Years later I attended York University in Toronto to study political science. I remember the day I had my first cup of coffee. On my way to a political theory lecture I passed Tim Hortons, a beloved Canadian doughnut franchise. I ordered two crullers, and the lady behind the counter asked me the question that changed my life.

"Would you like coffee with your doughnut?"

"You know what? I would. I'll take a cup of coffee."

I sat down in the courtyard and took a bite of the cruller. With a bit of the pastry still in my mouth, I sipped the coffee from a brown paper cup. It was exhilarating! The world suddenly became crisp, taking on a newfound clarity thanks to this magical drink.

I walked into the large auditorium, found a spot in the third row, and sat down. As the professor started lecturing, I became transfixed. *Wow! This political theory is so interesting!* Not only did I understand everything the professor was saying, I had my own ideas about what he was saying.

It took me giving up coffee for Lent to realize that caffeine was like a turbo that had been revving my brain for twenty-five years. When I took it away, my engine slowed down. The ideas came less quickly. And for the first time I realized the extent of my attachment to ideas and intellect. A great deal of my identity was caught up in my capacity to be intelligent. But I am not my thoughts. I am not my ideas. I'm separate from those things.

In the Gospels, Jesus tells us to love God with our heart, soul, mind, and strength (Mark 12:30). I've got the mind part down. However, not until I detach myself from my ideas can I understand that I am not just my mind. I can then begin the journey of learning to love God and people with my heart, soul, and strength as well.

How are we separate from our ideas?

How might our ability to think quickly help us avoid confronting our pain?

FREE TO LIVE FULLY

WE SEVENS LOVE OUR FREEDOM. Our pursuit of freedom is a gift to ourselves and others.

My friends Harmon and Jen have a four-year-old daughter named Fjola. I'm constantly flirting for attention from Fjola, who oscillates between disdain of my presence to tolerating my existence.

Earlier this year we celebrated my birthday at a local pizza joint called Via 313, which serves my favorite fancy deep-dish pizza in Austin. After dinner we decided to walk ten blocks down the road to Gemeli's, an Italian gelato bar. Fjola and I were walking next to each other. I asked her a few questions and she stared straight ahead, ignoring me.

After several minutes of me talking to Fjola—or really to myself—she grabbed my hand. I thought, *Oh, she's acknowledging my existence*! *Maybe she wants me to buy her some gelato*! Then ten seconds later she shook off my hand with vigor. I realized that we had crossed a driveway. Her parents were not nearby, so she had grabbed the nearest adult's hand. I was just a hand that asked her too many questions.

In that moment I thought about Fjola's growing capacity to cross the street. It had started with her parents carrying her across the street as a baby. Then, when she was a toddler, they walked her across the street. Now she understood that she could cross the street as long as she was accompanied by an adult. She didn't even have to like that adult. In time she would have the freedom to cross the street herself.

The Scriptures say that where the Spirit of the Lord is, there is freedom. You start with rules and structure that eventually free you to walk on your own.

I grew up in a fundamentalist tradition with so many rules it was hard to keep track. It was the opposite of freedom.

I can't play poker because it's linked to tarot, which is linked to witchcraft?

I can't listen to music with a beat because drumming is based on African music, which is linked to voodoo? (Isn't that kind of racist?)

I can't dance because it might lead to kissing, which will inevitably lead to premarital sex?

I can't smoke because it's not healthy, and yet we eat pizza, pancakes, and watered-down Kool-Aid every Sunday?

I can't curse because we're polite people, yet we talk behind people's backs and think those who don't believe like we do will burn in hell for eternity?

I can't watch movies in a theater because . . . ? I don't even have a reasonable explanation for that one.

I wonder if many religious folks see the restrictions and rules as the ends rather than a means to freedom and life. I wonder if many of us were taught not to cross the street *ever*. I wonder if we have been taught not to touch the stove so forcefully that we have never learned to cook.

Sevens are chasing freedom. We have the capacity and gift to lead the way to live full lives.

What does freedom look like for you?

When was the last time you felt free to be who you truly are? Where were you? Who were you with? What did you do? Why did you feel free?

What did the feeling of that moment teach you about God's Spirit?

FEELINGS?

SEVENS ARE THE ONLY ENNEAGRAM TYPE that isn't connected to the heart center. One of the ways this shows up
for me sometimes is having fun at the expense of others.

I recently recounted such a story to my boys.

"Your grandpa bought a house in a brand-new neighborhood in Toronto," I told them. "It was a new suburb, so
the edge of the town was still farmland. One night a chicken
wandered into the yard. Since Yeh-Yeh grew up on a farm
in China, he was used to catching chickens and eating them.
His first thought was, 'Oh, supper!' Since it was late at night,
he caught it and put it in a large box in the living room. He
was going to kill, clean, and eat it the next day.

"Well, the rest of us got home late that night. We all walked
into the house, went straight upstairs, and went to sleep. The
next morning your Aunt Rachel was the first to wake up. She
walked downstairs and saw a box in the middle of the living
room. Out of curiosity she opened the box."

"Oh my gosh. Then what happened?"

"What happened next was a live chicken burst out of the box with feathers flying everywhere! My sister started screaming and running. Our dog Barney heard the commotion and ran downstairs and of course started chasing the chicken around the house."

My boys were keeled over laughing.

"Then what happened?"

"Yeh-Yeh caught the chicken and put it back in the box."

"How about Auntie Rachel?"

"She was crying and went up to her room. Mah-Mah and Auntie Hannah consoled her."

"Did you eat the chicken?"

"We did, the next night. But your grandma pulled me aside and gave me specific instructions not to say anything about where the chicken came from. She said, 'Please don't tell your sister.'"

"So did Aunt Rachel ever find out?"

"Yes, three weeks later. We were sitting in church on a Sunday bored out of our minds. That day I was so bored I leaned over to Aunt Rachel and whispered in her ear, 'Hey, wanna hear something?'

"She said, 'Sure.'

"'Remember that chicken we ate a few weeks ago?'

"'The one that was super tasty?'

"'Yeah, that's the one. That was the chicken in the box that chased you.' And I smiled."

"What did she do?"

"She burst out in tears, punched my leg, and walked out of the sanctuary crying."

"Why did you do that?"

"To this day I'm not sure. I really thought it would be funny. I was bored and wanted a laugh."

"Wow. You're mean, Dad."

"I know. I felt bad."

The writer of Proverbs offers this nugget of wisdom: "Keep your heart with all vigilance, for from it flow the springs of life" (Proverbs 4:23 ESV). Part of my work as a Seven is to find my heart, live out of my heart, and walk with a heart open to the world around me. I'm slowly getting better at pausing to ask how my actions and words might make others feel.

Start a feelings note on your phone:

- Set an alarm to go off three times a day.

- In your Notes app, write down five emotions in response to this prompt: "Right now I feel . . . "

- Even if you can only say, "I think I feel _____ ," that's a good start.

SEVENS LOOKING FOR JOY

SEVERAL SPRING BREAKS AGO I went with some friends to Zion National Park in Utah. One of the hikes on my bucket list was Angel's Landing, a steep but breathtaking trek. Nine people have actually died while hiking Angel's Landing, and it just so happened that one of those deaths occurred the week before we were there. But I kept that fact to myself.

The hike itself doesn't look like much on paper. Five miles with a rise in elevation of fifteen hundred feet. I looked at the park description and wondered why it would take five hours. My friend Jason, my teenage boys, and I decided to take the challenge.

We woke up the next morning at 6 a.m. The shuttle dropped us off at the trailhead. The hike started off mild. It gained elevation slowly until we reached the base of the climb where the steep switchbacks began. We climbed steadily for a couple hours. Off in the distance I could see the tip of the mountain. Ant-sized people looked like they were standing on narrow slivers of rock. After the switchbacks, we started scrambling. Scrambling turned into sections that were so steep and narrow there were metal chains bolted to the rocks for us to hold. On both sides were five-hundred-foot drops.

"How are we allowed to do this?"

"What do you mean?"

"It feels like we should have at least signed a waiver."

"You're right."

"It feels like we could easily die."

"Last week someone did!"

"*What?*"

Oops. Did I say that out loud?

"Why didn't you tell us?"

"I didn't think you'd come with me."

"I'm too scared to be mad at you right now."

We continued climbing for an hour, then the trail flattened out before the climb got steeper again.

"Can we take a break?"

"Sure. Let's get some food and water in us."

We passed around the Nalgene and munched on some almonds. I could see the ant-humans traversing in the distance. The climb was about to get steeper and narrower. I felt a wave of anxiety rise in my body.

"Hey, guys, if we sit here any longer, my body might shut down in fear. Can we keep going?"

"Yeah, I feel the same."

"I can't remember the last time I felt this scared and had to force myself to continue."

We finally reached the top and had a 360-degree panoramic view of Zion National Park. One of the most stunning views I've ever seen. It took us another couple of hours to hike back down. We finally got to the lodge where our wives met us.

"So, how was it?"

"Uh . . . very exciting."

"Would you do it again?"

"Probably not."

We described the climb to them. But then I realized something. "You know what? Now that I'm talking about it and we've accomplished it, it was actually a lot of fun."

James 1:2 says we should "consider it pure joy" when we face challenges because it develops perseverance.

What is the difference between happiness and joy?

Why is it fun to do something hard?

What's something hard in your life now?

How might making it through give you positive associations down the road?

EXPECTATION BOXES

SEVENS DON'T LIKE TO GET BOXED IN. And I feel boxed in when I face the expectations of others.

My friends Gabe and Gina have a daughter named Chloe, and a few years ago they invited me to her first birthday party. It was on a Saturday afternoon, which left time for me to get a fifty-mile ride in before the event. When I arrived, I locked up my bike and took out my change of clothes.

Up to this point 100 percent of the one-year-old birthday parties I had attended were casual. Accordingly, my change of clothes was a vintage black T-shirt that ironically said, "I love you America!" (The irony is that I'm Canadian.) To complement that old T-shirt, I had some cutoff jean shorts and a pair of high-top white Vans. A good look for a Saturday barbecue but, I now know, not for a Korean one-year-old birthday. On this day I discovered that these events are as formal as a traditional wedding ceremony.

Still drenched in sweat, I walked from the bright sunlight into a candlelit restaurant foyer. I was wearing a cycling kit, with my change of clothes still in hand.

"Sir, may I help you?" the maitre d' asked.

"Um, I'm here for Chloe Ahn's birthday. Can you show me where your restroom is? I'd like to change first."

I washed up, threw my cycling kit into a tote, and walked back out into the restaurant. I saw a large sign near a private room that said, "Ahn birthday." Outside the room was a table with a seating chart. A kind, elderly Korean woman bowed to me. I responded with an even lower bow.

"What is your name?"

"Gideon Tsang."

"Ah, Pastor Gideon. The honored reverend." (I was dressed like a homeless person.) "You will be at table eleven."

The double doors opened into a banquet hall of families wearing ties and dresses. A three-year-old in a tuxedo walked by me. Why did it feel like everyone was looking at my thighs in my cutoff jean shorts?

Gina waved from across the room with a concerned look on her face.

Another friend, John, saw my outfit and started laughing. "Pastor Gideon. Not even business casual, eh? Casual casual? I take it someone didn't read the invitation."

"Dude, let me borrow your jacket."

"Ha! I'm six-four."

"No one will be able to tell once I sit down."

"You sure?"

"Totally."

To kick off the event, our host walked up to a microphone. "Welcome, everyone, to Chloe's first birthday," he said. "She's been God's biggest gift to us. To begin this celebration, I'm honored that my pastor came to celebrate with us. I'd like to invite him up to pray for us and give thanks to God. Please give a warm welcome to the Reverend Gideon Tsang!"

The room applauded. I got up out of my seat and noticed that John's jacket was longer than my shorts. I sheepishly walked to the front. It looked like I was wearing a suit jacket without any pants on.

"Let's, uh . . . thank God, um . . . Let's thank God for Chloe and the food. Please pray with me."

Most people in the room closed their eyes. The friends at my table were keeled over in tears trying to laugh without making a sound.

For my entire career this is what I've done to evade the traditional expectations placed on pastors. I've never had a business card. I don't have an office. I rarely dress up. I've never finished an email with my title or degrees.

Deep down I want to be seen as a fellow human being. I want what most people want: to be seen and known and loved for who I am—not what I do.

How do you feel about others' expectations of you?

In what ways do you evade those expectations?

How does it feel when you're genuinely seen and loved?

WHAT A SEVEN NEEDS

AS I WRITE THIS, we are in the middle of a global pandemic. The virus threatening public health knows no geographic, ethnic, gender, or socioeconomic barrier. We've lost folks along the way. Some of my friends own small businesses that might not survive the economic crisis.

For a Seven, much of this devastation is experienced socially. When I was part of a family of four and constantly around people with my work, I craved alone time. A movie or a meal alone with no one asking me questions felt like a slice of heaven. Now that I'm living on my own for the first time in twenty-five years, I've gone days without interacting with anyone. Boogie, my French bulldog, is my main conversation partner. He has a pretty face but honestly he's a bad communicator. I open my heart to him and he responds with a gurgly snort. Was that empathy or gas?

After the first week of the shelter-in-place policy, I was going stir-crazy. I compulsively looked at my phone, yearning for the electronic buzz of human communication. Even phantom buzzes were better than nothing.

Before this I had seriously been drawn to the idea of a monastic life. Could I be a Benedictine monk? In these last two weeks, it's been loud and clear: *absolutely not*. Monastic life is not compatible with being an Enneagram Seven.

In that second week of isolation I asked myself a question: How much social interaction did I need in a day? No longer did I have the luxury of going out and running into friends or having happy hours and parties lined up for months. I was looking at the possibility of another eight weeks of quarantine. This felt like being twenty miles into a two-hundred-mile bike ride. I felt fine now, but I was nervous about what my emotional state would be like in eight weeks.

The next day I called my friends Will and Keith for a FaceTime chat. They're both Sevens.

"How're you fellas holding up?"

"Man, this shit is too much."

"I'm so glad we moved to a larger house. We'd be in trouble if the four of us were still in five hundred square feet."

"Yeah, I couldn't handle being in the Airstream anymore. I'm at my parents'. How about you, Gid?"

"Honestly, it's been tough. I miss you guys. I miss running into each other."

We chatted for another twenty minutes. How was I feeling? A bit better. It was good to see each other's faces and laugh a bit.

My friend Jason called with an idea: "How would you feel about being quarantine buddies? As long as we don't see anyone else, we can hang out with each other."

"Are you asking me if I want to not see other people?" I asked.

"Pretty much."

"Deal."

He swung by later that afternoon. We smoked cigars, sipped whiskey, and watched *Tiger King* together.

That night it was my friend John's birthday. We had a forty-five-minute Zoom dance party scheduled. I jumped in a bit late and everyone was jammin' to "Bizarre Love Triangle." We danced and laughed. Boogie even came in for a couple of songs. With sweat dripping down my face, I blew kisses into the camera. "Happy birthday, Boo!"

I went to bed content that night. So I needed one FaceTime chat, one quarantine buddy, and a dance party. Those were my daily social needs. I wanted to judge myself for having more social needs than most. Then I remembered I was a Seven, not a Benedictine monk. And that was OK.

I fell asleep snoring in unison with Boogie.

As you complete these readings, what have you learned about what you need to feel OK? It might be related to human interaction or something else entirely. It might be something you think you shouldn't need.

What would it be like to acknowledge that part of yourself?

ENNEAGRAM
DAILY REFLECTIONS

SUZANNE STABILE,
SERIES EDITOR

Forty Days on Being a One
Juanita Rasmus

Forty Days on Being a Two
Hunter Mobley

Forty Days on Being a Three
Sean Palmer

Forty Days on Being a Four
Christine Yi Suh

Forty Days on Being a Five
Morgan Harper Nichols—Fall 2021

Forty Days on Being a Six
Tara Beth Leach—Fall 2021

Forty Days on Being a Seven
Gideon Yee Shun Tsang

Forty Days on Being an Eight
Sandra Maria Van Opstal—Fall 2021

Forty Days on Being a Nine
Marlena Graves